Hippies in

Our Midst

Hippies in Our Midst

The Rebellion Beyond Rebellion

By Delbert L. Earisman

Fortress Press   Philadelphia

© 1968 BY FORTRESS PRESS
Library of Congress Catalog Card Number 68-20163
6371L67   Printed in U.S.A.   1-2017

FOR PEGGY AND SCOTT

BECAUSE YOU'RE SO GREAT

Acknowledgments

I have incurred an overwhelming number of debts in the course of writing this book. I owe more than thanks to the young people who are the subjects of the book — not only to David, George, and Angel, who are named, but also to Gill, Nance, and others, many of whom are anonymous even to me. They all handed themselves over to me, and I hope deeply that I have been worthy of their trust by telling it the way it is.

I have had numerous conversations with colleagues who have helped me in formulating some of my ideas for the study. Evenings spent with Professors Wolfgang Zucker, John Wallhausser, and James Stam have been particularly helpful. President Carl G. Fjellman of Upsala College gave crucial assistance which made the actual writing of the book possible, and his secretary, Miss Ruth Brinkerhoff, was always warm and helpful. And I am grateful, finally, to the editors of Fortress Press who suggested to me that I might undertake this study for the Press.

I had always hoped to avoid the cliché situation of ending a page of acknowledgments with effusive gratitude to "the wife." But honesty forces me to cliché. My wife, Lucy, read the whole manuscript with a professional and scrupulous eye, arranged for typists, and, most important, lived through the whole experience with me when I had precious little time for quotidian domesticity.

DELBERT L. EARISMAN

Djakarta, Indonesia
January, 1968

Table of Contents

Introduction

One of the peculiarities of contemporary American culture is its interest in its young people, an interest that is not altogether healthy because it is a combination of both fascination and fear. One comes away from essays on rebellious youth in the popular periodicals such as *Life* or *Time* with the sense that adults in our society are looking for their young people to take them either to heaven or to hell. They tremble at the open outrages of Hell's Angels, at alleged free love among hippies and teeny-boppers, at widespread use of drugs, at the drunken parties of Long Island's young socialites, at the surfers' obsession with sun and danger; and, on the other end of the spectrum, they are shocked by draft-card and flag burning, the evidence, for some, of a young people too cowardly and unpatriotic to go to war. The shock with which society has reacted is exemplified by the legal savagery with which it has met what it sees as manifestations of rebellion. State after state is passing laws with astonishingly harsh penalties for use or possession of LSD; draft-card burners are getting increasingly long sentences; and police in Tompkins Square Park in New York City and in San Francisco have broken up essentially peaceful meetings of hippies with nightsticks.

On the other hand, there are an increasing number of adults who look at the more extreme young people of our country as perhaps offering a way out of a society that is becoming more and more difficult to live in sanely and productively. The success of these subcultures in the mass media is a real indication not only that adult

society is willing to be shocked but that it may be looking for substitutes for its own suburban reality and
middle-class tensions.

In general, journalistic accounts of deviant groups err
precisely in serving the need for shocking sensation or
for a new means of salvation; that is, they present these
young people in either their most grotesque or their most
ideal form, sometimes doing both simultaneously. A recent *New York Times* story illustrates this double tendency perfectly. The story, well-done on the whole, is about
a commune in New York's East Village run by a young
man called "Galahad." The account of the commune and
of Galahad is sympathetic. The article describes Galahad's taking home runaway teen-agers who had arrived
at the commune and his talking to the parents and the
child about the problems that had driven the child to
the commune. One mother reportedly said, "I've had no
trouble at all with Celia since Galahad talked with us."
On the other hand, the main picture accompanying the
article showed Galahad presumably high on LSD walking fearlessly along the top ledge of a six-story building.

The article itself was not essentially false — though I
suspect that the picture was faked, that is, that Galahad
was not high on LSD when it was taken, and I suspect
also that the reality of life in the commune was much
less attractive than the article would have it; in fact, the
commune was never really a "Digger" commune, as the
Times called it, and shortly thereafter it ceased to be a
commune at all. But because it was journalistic, the article tended to avoid two approaches to the phenomenon
that make it possible to think intelligently and humanly
about it, and thus it missed the whole point of the
phenomenon. These are the aspects that are illuminated

by personal involvement and historical analysis. The present work, then, is an attempt to describe and discuss a part of our present society from a personal-historical point of view, a point of view that should become clearer when I describe my method of work.

If we were to discuss an even wider range of groups in our society than space will allow, we could divide them in a way that they see themselves as divided, into activists and contemplatives, although I think that there are greater similarities between the two groups than the young people themselves would care to admit. Just as the quarrels between Leninist and Trotskyite Communists during the twenties and thirties often made them seem more bitter in their opposition to each other, at least on a verbal level, than they perhaps really were, so the two extremes of young people in our society tend to submerge their basic similarities. Still, there are crucial differences, and in emphasizing their differences the young people are closer to reality than those in the adult world who manage to lump all anti-war protesters together with drug-using adherents of beards and free love.

I use the terms "active" and "contemplative" quite deliberately to point to the parallel with the religious distinction made in the early church between the active way and the contemplative way — two equally valid ways of following the cross. This is precisely because I find that the underlying motivations of both types of young people are in the broadest sense religious. When I speak of religious motivation in this study I am referring to any conscious attempt to give meaning to life in terms of commitment to a self-transcending ideal. If the self-transcendent ideal is not called "God" in every case and if the attempt to find meaning is not called a "search for salvation," the difference may not lie so much in the nature of the activity itself as in the problems young people have with the language of their parents' generation. (In fact, the whole "Death of God" movement *may* be nothing more than evidence that we all have problems with the old language of faith.)

The contemplative groups to whom I shall limit my discussion are generally known as "hippies," a term whose connotations and journalistic uses make me want to put it in quotation marks every time I use it. But it is currency, though not very good currency, and so, with apologies to the diverse young people with whom I have talked and to their elders and teachers, I will simply use the word because there is no other — to use "love generation" would beg too many questions. There is also a growing group of young people who are generally known — though not by themselves — as "teeny-boppers." Because these take many of their ideals from the hippies and may, in some cases, be in a deliberately "pre-hippie" stage, I will consider them briefly. My focus will be on the phenomenon in the New York area, because that is where I could meet and talk to the young people themselves; but in many ways the spiritual center of hippie-dom is San Francisco. Still, movement by hippies between the two coasts is so constant that one meets many people from San Francisco in New York, and a New York view of things is not therefore totally invalid as a representative view.

This study, furthermore, is presented in full awareness that "the scene" changes rapidly. What was the case in the summer of 1967 will be different in the summer of 1968 — even some of the centers of the hippie sub-culture discussed here (like Galahad's) have in a notorious way already departed. Nevertheless, there is an identifiable phenomenon at hand — called the hippie — and we are well advised to find out what he really means.

As mentioned before, my method is both personal and historical, comprising the two dimensions of reality usually omitted from journalistic accounts. By "personal" I do not merely mean that I went to where the people were and talked with them warmly (I hope) and sympathetically in their environment. What I mean is best illustrated by something that was said to me early in my research. I had been in Tompkins Square Park talking to a couple of hippies, both well-educated, intelligent young men. As I was about to go, one of them said, "Be careful; you're looking into the vortex, and you can get dizzy; you may even fall in." That is, in opening myself to their style of life and even to their very mode of apprehending reality I became vulnerable to actually seeing it as a possible choice for my own life. It was a way of looking at a phenomenon from as close to the inside of it as I could get. There really was a possibility — at least a theoretical one — that I would decide to move my family down to the Lower East Side and share in the hippie life and hippie ethic. Similarly, when on other occasions I have talked to young activists, I have been tempted in some way to share their lives and their ideals, again involving a move out of suburbia into the slums where they do their work. If this book is at times a bit uncritical and even overemotional, it is the result of wanting to write at least some of it from that point of view, the point of view, that is, of the people about whom I write, as close as I could come to it.

My other focus, that of historical analysis, has been quite the opposite. One question this study will attempt to answer is: "Is what is happening today simply the perennial rebellion of young people against everything that their parents stand for or does it have some real cultural significance?" As I see it, the only answer to this question is an historical one, because nothing exists outside of the meaning of its own past. Admittedly, the ways of history are complex and deceptive. To establish a cause for a simple human act can, as any psychologist knows, be heartbreakingly difficult; to establish causes for a whole complex of human behavior is, in fact, impossible. One can, however, point to possible influences, tendencies, analogies, or parallels, and hope that the resultant net of circumstance will be fine-meshed enough to have caught some truth. But history involves more than discovering things in the past that lead up to the present. It involves seeing the way patterns in the present actually work. Thus, psychology and sociology are part of history — or should be part of history — and though I feel no degree of expertise in either of those fields an honest description of what is going on will propel me into those territories.

One final warning: this study will be biased in favor of the groups I am discussing, even though I shall try to be honestly critical about what is going on. It will be biased quite simply because in talking for hours on end to the subjects of the book I have gained a deep respect and affection for the genuine humanity of these young people and for their willingness to hand themselves over to me, to talk freely and openly about their deepest feelings. I feel defensive about them and even protective, perhaps, because they are not much older than my own children. I wish them well.

1.
At the Edge
of the Scene

Everybody has his own idea of Greenwich Village, depending on a lot of different things — his age, his social class, his prejudices, his job. A lot of it is historical. The Village used to be one of the Italian quarters of New York, and for many it still is. The people living above the shops and cafés and coffeehouses, leaning out of windows, calling their children in when the streets get crowded, are still the original inhabitants, "autochthonous," as the Athenians proudly called themselves, as though they had been created a special race right on that spot. The Italians are still evident, too, in the pizza parlors and in the grocery stores with ranks of olive oil cans and trussed and bulging cheeses and long, greasy sausages in the windows. It is the Italians, perhaps, who give the Village the kind of permanence and reality that keeps it from ever being just a cheap honky-tonk area. Spiritually, the Italians give the Village scene a deep glow of warmth and acceptance, so that whatever happens there or has happened there is far removed from a prudent, competitive Anglo-Saxon culture. To put it another way, the Village is an oasis of the Mediterranean sense of things and it will probably stay that way, even though the Italians themselves object most strongly to what they see happening now in the Village.

In the twenties, the Bohemians were in the Village. It was the art scene then, and that, too, remains, but is be-

1

coming weaker and weaker. There are still sidewalk portraitists who will do your portrait in pencil or charcoal for two or three dollars. There is still the outdoor art show in the spring, but the art is not good anymore; as much as anything else, it's the glossy, sentimental art of New England artist colonies, brought out to entice the tourist who is still stuck with an image of the Village of the twenties. Of course, there may still be artists — good ones — living in the Village, but they exhibit uptown, in the galleries in the fifties off Fifth and Lexington Avenues, and they are more likely to live across town in the "East Village" where rents are lower. Abstract expressionism, for example, is an East Village phenomenon. The artists used to go to the Village because it was once a place where one could live cheaply. But that passed a long time ago, except for the rent-controlled apartments, and getting one of those is almost impossible unless you have incredibly good luck. Some poets still live there, of course — E. E. Cummings did when he was alive — but they belong to an earlier generation.

A place like the Village always generates more than its share of phonies, hangers-on, charlatans. That is inevitable. But for large numbers of young people it is still the *scene.* The only way to see it and know it now is to go there, especially on a summer night, forget your dignities and prudences, forget everything you know about the way decent, civilized people ought to behave, and soak it up, stay with it, through an evening on until three or four o'clock in the morning, if possible — watching, listening, feeling, and hopefully accepting and understanding.

The Village of the guitarists and their girls, the incipient hippies and the teeny-boppers, is an incredibly small area including only a part of Washington Square

Park — roughly from the large fountain basin that never has water in it, on over to MacDougal Street, and extending up MacDougal Street for two or three blocks. It thins out quickly on the side streets meeting MacDougal, and two or three blocks away from the center of the action is the old Village, where men sit in bars watching the Yankees or Johnny Carson and where the ordinary homes of ordinary people are shut up tight after eleven o'clock. But in the center of the action is an immense crush of people. Underlying the strangeness, though, there should be, especially for older Americans, a strong sense of *déjà vu*, a feeling that you have been here before, because this is too much like the old county fairs to be dismissed as a completely new thing. The similarity is obvious on the surface: the food vendors — it's pizza and Italian sausage rather than chicken corn soup and hot dogs (there's even a balloon man); the immense crush of people (and though the people may complain about the crowds they instinctively, almost guiltily, wander back to those crowds if they find themselves very far away from the center of things); the courtship rituals; the sense of walking and walking, searching and searching; even the exhibits — how much difference is there between a man exhibiting his prize guernsey or a woman her prize asters, and kids exhibiting their long hair and beards or their netted legs?

But the real similarity, perhaps the crucial similarity, is the very deeply human motivation that brought them both into being. For the county fair was a time when people who had been isolated on their farms came into town to revel for a while in masses of flesh and noise and harmless self-indulgences. (My mother, who grew up on a farm in central Pennsylvania, recalls with nostalgia the

3

ways she would allot the quarter she had been given to spend at the Leonard's Grove picnic, and invariably she bought, among other things, a banana. Now bananas are the newest in psychedelia; it's all probably an irrelevant coincidence, but what *do* bananas represent, after all?) And in a sense, the guitarists and their girls may just be coming from loneliness to warm togetherness; from the loneliness of city apartments and suburban ranch houses, each on its own individual plot of ground, to a place where nothing is so real and so important as people, just masses of people.

There are differences, though, and the differences are real and may be basic. The first thing anybody notices is the hair on the men — long hair, often growing down over the shoulders. It looks dirty, too, and more often than not it is tangled and unkempt, though you occasionally see hair as carefully combed and brushed as any debutante's. Even beards are hardly noticeable in competition with the hair. Some of it is Beatle hair. Some looks more like the hair on pictures of Jesus, but nobody ever mentions that; the kids would be too embarrassed by the idea and their parents too outraged. I told one of the boys I talked to, an articulate kid from Pittsburgh, Pennsylvania, that people really found his hair offensive, were really upset by it, and he said, "You know, I feel very sorry for people who can only tell men and women apart by the hair." There's very little answer one can give to that. And who would dare to ask one of the boys why he doesn't get his hair cut and risk the inevitable return, "Why don't you let yours grow?" The point of all this is simple: when you start to let the Village really happen to you, you begin to learn more about yourself, your culture, and your assumptions than about the people who

4

flout them. If we are inclined to ask deep psychological questions about hair, we soon get embarrassed. We, not they, are the ones who pay two dollars every two weeks to get our hair cut. We are the ones who condemn ourselves to the really onerous job of shaving as soon as we get out of bed in the morning. Maybe, when it gets right down to it, the hair that offends us is a rich, innocent way of laughing at us.

There is really no Village uniform anymore, as there used to be a few years back. Any kind of shirt or jacket seems to do, and any kind of trousers — from the low-hanging, striped mod trousers, to tight jeans, to shorts. Some of the boys wear dirty white shirts with gaudy, flowered ties; some wear no shirts at all. Nothing they wear seems very fresh, but to a remarkable degree it expresses them individually, which is what it is intended to do. For the girls, the mini-skirts with net stockings come as close to a uniform as anything, but a lot of them are wearing the bell-bottomed granny pants; some are even wearing skirts of a more traditional length. Their hair tends to be long and straight but not particularly well-groomed. Loud colors predominate. Still, they are not the girls of the fashion ads. If they are attractive, and many are, the attractiveness is in their faces. Their clothes do not seem meant to allure but to express, even if what they express is nothing more than freedom from convention. The girls rarely wear makeup; a very few look as though they rarely wash.

There is, however, one basic difference between the boys and girls in the Village. A girl can come from a home in Queens, White Plains, or East Orange, New Jersey, and move into the Village scene for just an evening, reappearing the next day in the suburbs, just a nice

young girl. But since the real badge for the boy is the
long hair a boy cannot do that. You rarely see men with
long — really long — hair outside of the Village, even in
New York City. And so the boys belong, really belong
there, or they do not; and there's no way to disguise the
difference. Many of the girls, on the other hand, are
what are popularly known as "teeny-boppers." They do
live in the suburbs, or uptown, or in Brooklyn, and their
nightly or weekend escapes to the Village lack the finality
of the life of the boy who must let his hair grow for perhaps a year, which all the while makes life difficult for
him in any place but the Village.

Actually, of course, the guitarists and their friends and
the hippies are really only a minority of those in the
Village scene. There are at least four other groups add-
ing to the density of the crowds. First, in small numbers,
there are the residents, mostly sitting in the park. Those
who are visible in the evening are usually old people, sitting on benches, talking quietly and desultorily, just a
little bit away from the crowds but not too far away. One
such group of residents is the chess and checker players.
On the corner of the park closest to MacDougal Street
are about twenty chess and checker boards set in stone
tables between park benches. They have been there for
decades; and there the old-timers sit, with a following of
kibitzers, playing chess and checkers, surrounded by
bearded guitar- and bongo-playing youngsters and tourists, imperturbable, grandly dignified.

There are two kinds of tourists, the college kids and
the middle-aged gapers. The college kids are aggressively
clean — the boys scrubbed and shaved, often with coats
and ties on, and their girls, sometimes in shorts or mini-
skirts, and with that indefinable air of not belonging.

6

But they are what the cafés are really set up for, and they spend far more money in the Village than they would have at a nightclub uptown. They surround themselves with a protective wall of cleanliness and decency, as though they were walking through a zoo without cages. They rarely laugh, smile, or talk, as if opening their mouths might let in some of the contamination of the scene. The older tourists look more sympathetic. Who knows, they may have been rebels themselves, perhaps even relics of the Jazz Age, who find in the Village scene a bit of the careless, irresponsible gaiety that touched their lives so long ago. But they are uncomfortable because they don't belong either; and after they have been there for a while, they go to one of the bars that surround the area, sit among their own kind, and savor their complicated feelings of nostalgia, disgust, envy, and warmth.

At the lowest end of the scale in the Village are the derelicts, mostly Negroes. Many of them are clearly high, probably on heroin, but all of them are defeated, often collapsing on benches in Washington Square Park to sleep it off until the police move them along. They beg cigarettes or money from passersby, and they stop and talk, incoherently and sadly, to anybody who will listen. Sometimes one will become aggressive, but only by shouting in a blank, incoherent rage against a world in general.

Finally, there are the police — the *fuzz,* as the kids call them — in sufficient numbers to make them a real part of the scene. They stand around in pairs, six or eight to a block, keeping people moving, breaking up spontaneous little concerts in the park, checking the licenses of the vendors, directing traffic. They are al-

7

most all young, weary, and bored. The kids hate the police, and the police have little tolerance for the kids; they are capable of jabbing them with nightsticks and calling them queers or parasites just to keep them from standing too long in any one place.

Sensations in the Village are more intense than elsewhere. You see a good-looking boy with curly blond hair, perhaps about twenty — not a hippy — shuffling dully by, eyes glazed, a livid scar on his forehead, evidently on a heroin high, in some set of drug sensations all his own. Or on a stoop outside of a store a young father, long-haired, bearded, dirty, barefoot, holding his arm around his young son, equally dirty. But it looks strangely like a kind of very deep love. A boy walks by with a daisy in his top shirt buttonhole. The daisy reminds you of the letters chalked seven feet high on the pavement in the park, reading, "Flower Power."

One of the strange parts of the revolution going on here, if it is a revolution, is the prominence of flowers. During the Spring Mobilization for Peace on April 15, 1967, there were daffodils everywhere. Bearded boys and mini-skirted girls carried huge bunches of daffodils and gave them to the marchers and to anybody else who would take them. The term "flower power" is also connected with the most vivid impression one takes away from the Village — a haunting memory of the eyes of the guitarists and their girl friends. There is no reason to think that their eyes should be any bigger than anybody else's. Nothing biological or sociological supports it; but the impression remains that the eyes glowing out from the matted hair are large and soft. There is a strange beauty in those kids' eyes, like the beauty of the eyes of some forest animal. But the eyes

8

look vulnerable, perhaps hurt. Maybe when we get to understand these kids better, we'll find that their secret is in the hurt that glows from their eyes but that they mask everywhere else. In talking to them I got some indications of that, in fact.

If flowers are one part of the revolution, buttons are another. By this time everybody knows about the buttons. Their style and message are much the same as literate graffiti, a combination of wit, obscenity, scatology, and protest. They are, of course, manufactured by companies that hope to make a great profit from them, and one cannot always be certain that they are authentic representations of the feelings and thoughts of the kids. Maybe they are there for tourists, after all, but some of the kids do wear them, and they do seem to express the style of the kids. Many of the buttons deal with drugs and combine the advocacy of psychedelic drugs with protest against the war: "LSD not LBJ"; "Burn pot, not people." A few combine protest with anti-clericalism: "Kill a Commie for Christ." Some are frankly hedonistic and self-indulgent as well as rebellious: "Pornography is fun"; "If it feels good, I'll do it"; "Cunnilingus." And some are what we might think of as existential: "Is there life after birth?"; "I am a human being; do not fold, spindle, or mutilate."

Like the buttons, the cafés are commercial, now cater largely to tourists, and may represent the kids only tangentially. But the cafés do, at any rate, form a nucleus for the crowd. Perhaps they're like the exhibits at the county fairs: they are the ostensible reason that people go where they go and they do express something about the people, but not as much as journalism would have us believe. They have names like "Café Wha?" (one of the older

9

ones), "The Underground," "Café Freudian Slip," "Café
Feenjon" *(feenjon* is Arabic for *cup).* They do not sell
alcoholic beverages because most of their clientele are
under twenty-one, and they couldn't get licenses anyway
from city officials, who are already ambivalent about
them. They have replaced the coffeehouses and the jazz
clubs as places of popular resort, though the coffeehouses
and the jazz clubs — Village Vanguard, even Tony Pas-
tor's — are still there.

The cafés are noisy, gaudy, provocative. The "Underground" advertises, "Join the Lunatic Fringe. Love in.
Naked Freak-out." They are expensive. The first night
we went in, we decided to try the Café Wha? Down-
stairs there was a sign, $2.50 cover per person; you must
buy at least one drink. But when we started out again,
unwilling to pay so much for so little, one of the managers came up and told us he would let us in for the
student rate of $1.50 each. Inside we were seated at one
of a row of benches surrounding the stage on three sides,
and a waitress in a low blouse and tights — but wearing
a cross on a chain around her neck — brought us a menu
with items on it like "Rum Rocket" for $1.75 each. We
ordered Rum Rockets, which were large, cold, and deli-
cious; but there was no rum in them.

The band that was playing was one of the pop bands
that marks the center of the life of the kids we had gone
in to see. There was a drummer, two guitarists, an accordianist, and a singer who had a tambourine. All the
instruments were wired to large amplifiers and every
member of the band sang into a microphone three inches
from his mouth. The stage was lit by a battery of colored
theatrical lights that kept changing so that it was alter-
nately bathed in blue, red, and green. Sometimes pure

10

white spots were flashed off and on, giving a stroboscopic effect, so that the performers were caught in a series of instantaneous, non-continuous still shots.

What happens is the total experience that is characteristic on the one hand of the phenomenon known as "McLuhanism," and on the other of the psychedelic experience. The music is not merely loud; it penetrates you. You hear it with your legs, your thighs, your belly, and your bowels. Even the lights have more than a merely visual effect; you do not see what is happening, you happen, too — all of you. More than anybody else the musicians are caught up in it. Their hair is only slightly longer than the Beatles', but they are younger, less mocking, more enthusiastic. When they play, they play with their whole bodies, giving themselves up to a kind of ecstasy. But it's a cool ecstasy, if such a thing exists. At the end of a piece, sweaty and panting, they smile warmly and easily, almost as if to say, "It wasn't all quite for real. We meant part of it, but we weren't all that serious. It is a great game, after all." Underneath the ecstasy and the easy smiles, though, there is a childlike, lovable quality that comes through strongly and is probably, everything else considered, what turns their fans on so intensely. They have never lost the essential innocence of children. And if their hair is long it might as well have been because they just forgot to go to the barber as because they are rebelling in some way or another. The accordianist, especially, has a saintly look about him. He alone smiles rarely, and he tends to have a strained, tortured look on his face. He could have been the model for a painting of Saint Sebastian, that sweet, forbearing boy, punctured by the arrows of the heathen for the greater glory of Christ.

11

In talking to any of these boys, one finds that his music is to him the most serious thing in his life. Most of them have poured all of their earnings into new equipment, new guitars and amplifiers. They spend their days practicing together; some of them, unable to read music, listen to records of the Beatles or the Rolling Stones or the Monkees, take off from them, and then go on to their own arrangements and their own songs. One boy we talked to had quit school — a state college in western Pennsylvania — to come to New York to work for a publisher and live in the Village, all for his music. His only political views were that he hated and feared the draft because it would interrupt his music.

Like the jazz musicians of an earlier age, though, they are curiously inarticulate when asked to talk about the music itself. It is perhaps too close to them, too private, too much their way of some kind of ultimate self-fulfillment to be talked about. I don't think that they talk about it much even to each other. They play it, with their strange, lovable, mocking ecstasy that defines about as well as anything else the mood and spirit of young America today, or at least the part of young America that this book will deal with.

So much for the setting. My goal was to go to the kids themselves, to let them speak for themselves, where they were and where they felt most intensely alive. At about nine o'clock in the evening the little girls start to move onto the scene. They usually come in twos, some slanting across the park from the subway station, some getting out of taxis, some even being let out of private cars. Mostly mini-skirted, they begin their cruising. When a middle-aged square begins to talk to them they are at first suspicious, but soon become talkative and eager.

Their ages range from sixteen to eighteen and they come from both New York City and the suburbs. Like the guitarists, they can be self-deprecatory, even cool. When you ask them why they are there they admit that there really isn't as much doing as it looks. One girl, more sophisticated than most, said, "We do nothing. That's it. Just nothing. But if we didn't come, we'd sit home and feel, well, kind of unfulfilled, as though something might be going on and we weren't there." When asked why they are there, they point to the fact that there is no place else to be. One young man said, "You know, they don't make playgrounds for us." A couple of the girls liked it because the people there weren't phonies. By that she meant that people could dress the way they wanted, wear their hair the way they wanted. Another pointed to the lack of obligation. Nobody there expected anything from them. They went home late. The exodus didn't start until after midnight, and many stayed until three or four o'clock in the morning — for the most part still cruising, still stopping to talk briefly to friends, and then walking along some more.

Most of them gave a general impression of intelligence. They talked well, fluently and grammatically, without slang and without profanity. That might have been because they weren't talking to one of their own, but I suspect that the tendency to think of these young people as having a special language of their own that they use constantly to the bewilderment of outsiders is one of those non-facts that makes good newspaper and magazine reading. Like any square trying to be hip, I called marijuana *pot*, which they did, too; but I called LSD *acid*, which they understood, but they called it *LSD*. Even if their language and general conversational demeanor were

13

standard American, however, they lacked — more than almost any other young people that I know — the standard American goal-orientation. Rarely were they planning to go to college. They had not liked school, and college didn't make any more sense than school had. Their occupational plans were simple. They were going to be secretaries, or beauticians, or they simply didn't know. Because the bands are almost all male the girls could not, like many of the boys, aspire to make it big in the pop music world. In general, we tend to condemn young people who don't have specific plans that they're working for; it's a basic part of our whole cultural attitude. And it is true, even beneath cultural attitudes, that one condition for human self-fulfillment is to be working towards something productive. A human being is not made to drift, to seek the pleasure or escape of the moment. The children of past generations were brought up on "Life is real, life is earnest, and the grave is not the goal," and even if the tone is strident there is still truth in it.

Perhaps one of the keys to the attitudes of the kids is the blank I drew when I asked them about politics. If you press them, they're against the war. But they are aggressively non-involved. Politics is perhaps most real to them in the presence of the policemen standing ready to tell them to move on or to stop their guitar-playing, but, as one boy put it, "never in sight when something serious might be about to happen to us." (Some of the middle-class tourists do get rough and abusive when they're drunk.) These kids, then, are not the protestors against Vietnam or against racial injustice (racially mixed couples are common and accepted in this part of town, so that down here they can avoid the hard facts of

14

acial injustice elsewhere). They probably don't know
he names of their local senators and representatives. At
east one did tell me, though, that he was scared. He
hought he lived in fear of what society would do to itself
and to him. It was more than war; it was just a sense of
error in the air that was perhaps projected onto the
policemen more than the policemen actually deserved.
Another had a general sense, nothing specific, but as he
alked, it seemed as though the Village was almost like a
ghetto to him. They were there because, being what they
were, there was nowhere else for them to be.

These kids in the Village are in many ways real drop-
outs, even though they often return home. Like their
older brothers the hippies, they protest by refusing to
belong. It's a silent, inchoate protest, and if you ask any
of them if they feel they are rebelling or revolting against
something, they look blank. But ultimately there is no
form of protest so profound as simply saying "No."

The sensational part of their lives, of course, is the use
of psychedelic drugs. The young people I talked to did
not use any addictive drug such as heroin, had no interest in it, and considered it something that belonged in
the slums, where its use grew out of despair and generations of suffering and deprivation. The drug they uni-
versally had used was marijuana, often called *pot* and
sometimes *grass*. Most said they could take it or leave
it; the experience was not a bad one, but they did give
me the impression that it wasn't such a big deal either.
One did say that pot had become a hang-up for her for
a while, but then she had stopped taking it. That did
not mean it was physiologically addictive but rather that
she had come to have a psychological dependence on
either the drug or the context in which it was taken.

15

Most had taken LSD, though they were aware that LSD was dangerous. One boy said that he was glad it was illegal and thought it should never be legalized but that he planned to continue taking it occasionally. But even if they were aware of the dangers of LSD, their attitude towards it was remarkably casual. They knew about the dangers of psychosis and hoped that it wouldn't happen to them; they knew about "bad trips," when all of one's fears and anxieties were magnified into profound depressions and sufferings, and so learned that there are certain frames of mind in which you don't take a trip. Perhaps, though, the one thing that can take the sensationalism out of the fact that they all smoke pot and that most have tried or will try LSD is their almost total disinterest in the drug of their parents' generation — alcohol. None, so far as I could tell, were teetotalers; they just couldn't care less about liquor.

All of the young people I talked to said that their parents knew they were there and were not particularly concerned. Their attitudes towards their parents are perhaps well under the surface, but I have heard far more hostility towards parents from good college students or from people of my generation than I heard from the guitarists and their girl friends. The one girl I talked to who indicated real problems between herself and her father explained them by saying that she and her father were too much alike. One boy said that he loved his parents very much and that they loved him. One girl, though, an extremely perceptive and sophisticated girl, talked a lot to us about love. It was not all fresh and spontaneous because she admitted that she had known a psychologist quite well (he was a friend; she had not been in therapy). But her analysis, if trite, may still have

16

been true enough: "There's not enough love," she said. "If we had had enough love in our homes, if the parents uptown had given us more love, maybe we wouldn't have to come down here. All of this, the sex, the drugs, the be-ins, all of it is a way to try to have a kind of universal love because we haven't been able to learn to love as individuals."

But she was not the only one talking about love. Love, like flowers, is a ubiquitous symbol of their life. "Make love, not war" is not simply an invitation to free love — though nobody is quite sure what it is an invitation to. There is, indeed, a sense in which love has replaced sex as a significant value. One doesn't, of course, ask seventeen-year-old girls whether or not they're virgins and, if they are not, the details of their sexual lives. One did tell me that our generation was obsessed with sex. Another said that if the rest of your life was warm and honest, your sex life would be, too. They all expressed a much more casual attitude towards sex than towards music or drugs. Certainly they are more casual than the young people grimly living up to the official codes. I remember from my own college days the intense, pained discussions of the whole subject. They are right; we are obsessed with sex. They, so far as I could tell, merely enjoyed it. Marriage, too, did not really interest them one way or another. A few of the girls valued freedom very much and did not plan marriage for a number of years. Certainly their relations with men now were not courtship. As for the kinds of mates they wanted, their answers were remarkably similar: they didn't know; they knew only that he would be a person who as an individual they, as individuals, would love. One boy, asked what he thought was the difference between the sexual standards

17

of his generation and those of ours, said, almost sullenly, "Well, it's like this. Maybe your standards worked for you. They wouldn't for us." That was one of the few pieces of unconscious irony I had heard all evening.

The newspaper term for the kids I talked to is "teeny-bopper." But it's part of the marvellous richness and diversity of people anywhere that newspaper reports can never really get it the way it is. No one that I talked to admitted to being a teeny-bopper, a term they defined in various uncomplimentary ways and had, they admitted, been applied to them. Maybe they had been teeny-boppers — one girl admitted that, too. But whatever giggly, conforming, empty-headed phenomenon the term describes, it is simply not to be admitted to in the Village these nights.

2.
The Love
Generation

The ads read, "The East Village Is What's Happening."
And they're right. The West Village, the Village of the
teeny-boppers, the sidewalk art shows, and the coffeehouses, is still alive, still crowded night after night in the
summer, still exciting. But if you walk crosstown to the
East Side, you'll find that the new things, the important
things, are happening over between about Third Avenue
and the East River, centering on Tompkins Square Park.
The East Village even has its own newspaper, the *East
Village Other* — more "hip," more drugs and sex, a mystic-
oriented *Village Voice* (the new thing of a decade ago).
The East Village itself is rawer and less mellow than the
West Village. There are no gracious old brownstones,
few of the trees and shrubs that soften the West Village,
and little sense of tradition. The streets are lined with
trash and many of the buildings have been vacated, their
windows broken, the front doorways boarded shut. The
area even lacks the kind of utter squalor that would
allow one to label it a slum. Ethnically it is Eastern
European, Ukrainian, and Polish, with large numbers of
Negroes and Puerto Ricans who have recently moved in.
Along the side streets, though, are the hippie shops —
bright, even gaudy, little shops — selling mod clothes,
beads, books, and the posters and other paraphernalia of
psychedelia. The proprietors of the stores are young,

19

long-haired, beared kids, who manage to merge the capitalistic instincts with hippie culture. Hippies are now New York's newest tourist attraction.

The American tendency to commercialize everything, even to vulgarize it, makes it hard to ever get to a thing itself. And so now that the hippies have been discovered by the press and the tourists they will become surrounded by fakes of all sorts; they will be sensationalized, over-praised, psychologized, damned, imitated. The hippies themselves are conscious that they are a tourist attraction and are amused by the fact. One explained to me that the tourists all go down to Tompkins Square Park on Sunday afternoons and stare at the hippies sitting on the grass inside a low iron fence. But he pointed out that the fence worked both ways — if the tourists were staring at the hippies, the hippies were looking back at "straight" society, both amused and saddened.

But first, some definitions. *Hippie,* though a journalistic term more than one the hippies themselves tend to use, is not rejected by them in quite the way "teeny-bopper" is rejected by the young people who are likely to be called that. (The hippies themselves tend to be some-what contemptuous of the teeny-boppers, who differ mainly from hippies in that they go home at night to their parents' houses, a very crucial difference.) One very articulate hippie told me that they think of them-selves as the Love Generation or the Flower Generation — probably a little pretentious. In general, a hippie is a young person — though some are easily over forty — who is consciously rejecting the symbols and values of middle-class civilization in order to become self-sufficient by re-ducing his needs to an absolute minimum. This, as much as anything else, accounts for the unkempt appearance, since haircuts and shaves are clearly not necessary except as symbols of respectability. Furthermore, the hippie ethic, which I will write more about later, almost always involves their version of love, which is a more or less passive sense that everybody is a peculiar individual with his own particular "thing" — interest, attitude, understanding of reality — and that one should try to understand and accept other people's "things" without trying to put one's own thing on somebody else. And finally, hippies are united around the psychedelic drugs, particularly LSD. They almost all take marijuana, too, but marijuana has a relatively weak, uninteresting effect for them, and no style of life seems to grow out of marijuana as grows out of LSD.

When I first walked into Tompkins Square Park, it was shortly before July 4, and firecrackers were exploding at intervals in the park, set off to harass the hippies by the Negro and Puerto Rican children who dislike them. At a particularly loud explosion I jumped, startled, and noticed a hippie sitting alone on a bench and smiling at me, not in mockery but in the amusement of good fellowship. We had established a sort of communion by that, and I went to talk to him. He was dressed in mod clothes, a bright blue paisley shirt and striped trousers, all immaculately clean. (The idea that all hippies are dirty is simply not true. Some perhaps are, but most were perfectly clean, with clean clothes and hands. Only the feet tended to be dirty, because hippies often wear sandals or go barefoot and in New York during the summer anybody's feet will get dirty if he keeps them exposed. Perhaps hippies look dirty because anybody who lets his face get surrounded by hair and who wears drab old clothes will look dirty from a distance. I myself think

21

that the myth of hippie dirtiness expresses more about our culture than about those who drop out.) My friend had long curly red hair and a red beard, and looked rather cherubic on the whole. He was also older than most of the hippies (twenty-nine) and had a copy of the *New York Times* on the bench beside him. In short, he was not typical in a number of ways. Because he was writing in a notebook, I suspected that he might be doing the sort of thing I was, only going in for it more completely; but I was wrong. He was a hippie, and if he was not typical no hippie will ever claim to be typical or to speak or live for anybody but himself.

He introduced himself as David, and he was extremely articulate and well-educated. He had a master's degree and had published with a major New York firm; he was far from rejecting either of these facts of respectable life. At the time I met him he was in the midst of writing a long letter to a friend, trying to explain his first LSD trip,* which he had taken about a week previously; it was a matter of trying to put into words the inner facts of the experience itself. He tried over and over to explain it to me, even though he also said that before you take LSD you want to take it so that you can tell about it, but then after you take it you lose all ability to talk about it. But when trying to say what the trip was like, he consistently — and this is true of most hippies — used religious concepts and terminology. He found the ex-

---

* Hippies have a limited amount of slang that they use regularly. But, like all good slang, it is connotatively precise and should really be defined by use in a number of contexts. Their slang includes words like *trip, straight,* or, rarely, *square, turn on, thing,* or *bag,* and various terms for their drugs. Hereafter I will without apology use hippie slang where appropriate without quotation marks.

pression "God is in a sugar-cube" extreme and vulgar, and he was careful to point out that the experience was not religious in any sense ordinarily understood by straight society. But the feelings were those of being in communion with a whole, of loving and wanting to share, a sense that God was there, was everywhere, was among men, was men, that one was God. It was, he said, the most intense religious experience of his life — and he had been reared as a Catholic. In spite of his feelings, however, his behavior had been somewhat bizarre. David said that he liked the color blue and had surrounded himself with blue objects. It came to him during the trip that he wanted to paint his feet blue. So he did. But then he asked himself why he should be doing a thing like painting his feet blue, and he answered himself, "Why shouldn't I paint my feet blue?" He said, too, that he felt as if he were all energy — that everything in the world was energy, that God was energy, and that he was energy, and that he could use the energy any way he wanted.

The after-effects of LSD, he explained, quite simply allow you to concentrate on what is really important and to forget about what is unimportant. He pointed out how much emotional energy all of us spend worrying about things that aren't important — whether we left the car door locked or not — and that after taking LSD he stopped worrying about anything that wasn't really important or that he couldn't do anything about.

David had been a slow convert. It had taken him perhaps six years to get to the point where he was and he still had some vestiges of straight culture — his clothes, for instance, and his inability to do without the *New York Times*. Earlier in his life he had once bought

twelve hundred dollars' worth of clothes and then discovered that he was holding down two jobs to support
his clothes. He was also one of those people who had
wanted to write a book but couldn't get time away from
work to write the book and so found himself in the typical middle-class bind. He wanted creativity, but he was
owned by his possessions, and, unable to give them up,
he lost himself. Actually, David cheated just a bit. He
got a job that required almost no work and wrote his
book on company time. He talked a great deal about
sharing. All hippies did, and whenever I was with a
hippie who had anything — a coke, a sandwich, a can of
beer — he automatically and without any self-consciousness offered me some of it.

David had been impressed by the spiritual poverty of
middle-class culture, he said, when he was on his first
full-time job, teaching in a school in a New York slum
area. Visiting the home of one of his students, he noticed
that a hungry little boy came to the door. The family
invited the boy in and fed him, and he left. Nobody
knew where he came from, where he was going, who he
was. But they fed him. David had grown up in the
suburbs in an area of sixty-thousand-dollar homes, and
he remembered that when the neighborhood children
were playing together at one of their houses and lunch-
time came, the mother of the boy at whose house they
were playing would send all the other boys home to their
own mothers for lunch. "They weren't even strangers,"
he said. "They were my friends; we were there playing
together, and yet in those sixty-thousand-dollar houses
the people who had all the money just never thought of
sharing a simple little thing like a lunch, and down in

the slums anybody would share their food with you if you asked them."

He went on from there to a denunciation of suburbia, about which he was strongly emotional. To him suburbia represented not only selfishness, but the de-masculinization of the male who spent his day working at uncreative and unrewarding work in order to keep a large house and lot that he came home to from the city too late to enjoy. The father was also too tired and away from home too much to give his children the love and care that boys particularly need from fathers. It was comments such as these from many of the hippies, more than anything they said about themselves personally, that revealed just why they were there.

I asked David whether he had ever thought about any historical precedents or analogies for the sort of thing that was going on with the hippies. He pointed out first that a large number of primitive peoples had used drugs for religious reasons, and that even in the Western world the use of hallucinogenic drugs had only been done away with by Christianity. But he also pointed to the Bogomils, an obscure heretical sect in ninth-century Bulgaria that had dropped out — refused to participate in the society of that time. Bulgaria, like the major powers today, had become militarily strong and aggressive, engaging in war after war. But the members of the sect attracted others and soon people had dropped out of the society in such large numbers that Bulgaria was no longer important militarily.

Like all other hippies, David practices free love; that is, he will stay with a girl for a while, perhaps a matter of months, and then they will separate and find other partners. He assumes that sometime he will find a girl that he likes well enough to stay with permanently, and then he will marry her. But he also feels that his present style of life has removed all of the sexual tensions and anxieties that usually plague Western man. David felt that birth-control pills were working a tremendous social revolution — he thought that from junior high school on every girl ought to be given the pill, whether she wanted to take advantage of it or not. I saw David later that evening, strolling in the park with his girl friend — he called her his roommate — and they were casually talking and holding hands like any straight couple.

Later when I walked up to a group of four hippies sitting on the grass, they were clearly frightened. They saw me coming and pretended not to notice, but they stiffened and finally looked up with real fear. My asking them if they would talk to me for a few minutes didn't relax them any, and throughout our conversation they kept reminding me that though I seemed okay they had no way to be sure I wasn't a detective or a narcotics officer. But finally they did relax, and talked willingly. There was a married couple, twenty and twenty-two, and two single boys, each twenty. All had had some college, and one, at least, was considering returning to college. They had all come from middle-class homes, though one was aware that his parents had come recently from the lower class up into the middle class. The married boy talked most freely, a great deal of his talk being about religion. He was constantly aware of God and specu-lated freely about the after-life. He said that he thought that perhaps this was hell — this earth — and that after this life we would all have been punished enough to go on to a better life. But he was certain, at any rate, that something so precious as a human being would live on, somewhere, somehow. When I asked them to define love one of the other boys started talking, and I caught out of the corner of my eye the young couple holding hands and smiling at each other to show me that *that* was their definition of love. They planned to have children sometime, but only when they could afford it, and they had already given thought to the future of their children. The girl guessed rather sardonically that their children would probably rebel against them by becoming bankers or something; but more seriously, she was determined that she must let her children find their own things, their own styles of life, without her interfering and controlling. She, by the way, would not have been taken for a hippie anywhere but in Tompkins Square Park unless one noticed that she had no shoes on. She wore a bright white T-shirt and neat gray striped slacks. Her hair was, well, ordinary, and her whole demeanor and look were those of a bright, moderately attractive American girl. They were young, of course, and they were trying to impress me with the goodness of their life; but all the same, I have rarely seen married couples with such evident and strong love for each other. Even the two boys who were with them occasionally looked over proudly at this love. They said that they had been married for the "squarest of square reasons": they wanted to say that they belonged to each other in front of an altar of God.

Of the other two boys in the group, one had been planning to become a minister; he felt that by living the life he was currently living he was still involved in a religious thing, but more deeply and with less distraction than if he had been a minister. The other boy had a strange smile on his face most of the time that I was

talking to the others. He said little but turned to me
again and again with the smile that I thought might
have been a mocking one. He could have been just coming off a trip, or perhaps still on one — I didn't then
know the facial expressions associated with drugs. But
just as I was about to go, he started talking about the
book I had told them I was writing. He thought that I
should stay with them longer, find out more about their
real motivations for being there, get to know them emotionally, not just with a series of questions, because what
they were doing was essentially an emotional thing and
couldn't be talked about very well. I still don't understand his smile, which was more than anything else like
the smile on archaic Greek statues that scholars tell us
is the smile of innocent contentment. But I know that
he wasn't mocking me. I had gone as far as I had dared
to go in plumbing the minds and hearts of these young
people, and he was inviting me further. I had heard that
hippies did not like to talk to members of straight society;
I had been warned to expect to be "put on" — spoken to
half-seriously, half-derisively. But they were all without
exception talking enthusiastically, trying to explain to me
what it was like. One boy who was going to the Haight-
Ashbury section of San Francisco had taken my name so
he could write to me about what it was like out there.
And here was one inviting me to search his feelings any
way I could, who deeply wished for me to understand
him. The reason lay, perhaps, in the fact that I presented myself as simply and unashamedly straight — I was
middle class and approaching middle age, and I had not
smoked marijuana nor taken LSD. That is, in every respect but one I represented their parents' class and generation. The one respect in which I was different was

that I was sitting on the grass in Tompkins Square Park, seriously listening to them. And they could tell me what they could not tell their own parents — that they took LSD, that they practiced free love, and that in spite of the way it might seem to the parents it was for the kids something religious and moral and the realest thing in the world.

It was not, really, that the young people felt that they had been unloved nor that they did not love their parents. Most of them said that they did love their parents, very deeply. But they could not communicate with them, and perhaps never had been able to. The married girl said that she knew her parents loved her but that they had never understood her. Their hunger to talk to me, then, was a part of the hunger they had to really talk to their parents, possibly a hunger that had been developing for nineteen or twenty years out there in a thirty-thousand-dollar house in a suburb.

It is, after all, almost sad, because for the most part hippies are younger than they seem. From a distance they look older than they are because of their long hair and beards and bizarre clothes, but when one talks to them one soon begins to feel towards them as one feels towards any young person. In their gentleness and innocence they begin to seem even younger than they really are. Like the teeny-boppers, they have the habit of giving their age to their next birthday. To "How old are you?" they say, "I'll be twenty in October."

I spent most of my time one evening talking to a group of two boys and a girl who were sitting on the grass listening to the "Blues Project," a series of bands performing in the Tompkins Square Park bandstand. Both boys had gone to college and both had left partly because they were forced to take courses that had no relevance to what they planned to do or to their own sense of themselves. But both planned to go back or to find a college that would not force them to take irrelevant courses. One was planning to become a marine biologist. He planned, in fact, to continue living the kind of life he was living now, including drugs and self-awareness — even, I suppose, the beard and the long hair — when he was a marine biologist. He represents, perhaps, one aspect of the hippie world that is most likely to have real influence on American culture in the future, because there is no reason that a person cannot be a hippie and at the same time work at most productive jobs in our society. The psychedelic drugs do not disable people once a trip is safely over, and hippies, contrary to general opinion, are not averse to work as long as it's work they choose for their own reasons and not work foisted on them by the demands of society or status. The same boy disapproved of colonies of hippies moving out into the country to live a simple, tribal existence in nature. His colonies would have scientists, teachers, doctors — even, for that matter, industrialists and managers. He didn't want a static, self-contented world; he wanted a progressive world.

The other boy was an artist and a poet. His particular thing, however, was awareness. He liked to watch, to listen, to soak up the world around him for his art and his poetry. He was convinced that LSD made him a better artist because, under its influence, he had become aware of aspects of reality that he had not been aware of before. He explained it as suddenly seeing a person in a new way, several new ways, seeing things about the person that had been there all along but that he hadn't seen. Then, when reality was enriched for him, he could evaluate and choose, and not simply accept the same old fixed sense of things that he'd had before. And so LSD was for him not a dulling sensation, or even a vast profound thing, but a sharpening up of sensations that gave the mind more power to choose, to evaluate, even, perhaps, to reason. What he didn't know was that he was saying what some of the most important and brilliant existential philosophers and some of the most exciting new psychotherapists have been saying about the fully human personality for years.

He, more than any other hippie I talked to, talked about love, particularly in relation to God. He had been a Wisconsin Lutheran, but what he had now was far more valuable to him than his Lutheranism had ever been. God was a being simply bursting with love, loving so much that he created men just for something more to love. "I know," said the boy, "why I was created." I knew the answer before it came: "To love." But even he was having problems. Several weeks previously, the Tompkins Square riots had taken place. ("Riots" is a newspaper term. According to the hippies and even according to some official reports a police tactical squad had, with no more provocation than laughing resistance to orders to get off the grass, run savagely into a group of hippies, with nightsticks swinging.) He had seen and — most sickeningly — heard nightsticks hitting human skulls. A friend of his, a pregnant girl, had had a miscarriage after being kicked by the police. He finds it hard to love the policemen. He'll try though. He at least is not a fanatic of love in the sense that he lives and loves with no uncertainty about what he is doing.

I met David again some days later and talked to him

31

briefly. He had just been on his second trip and was most excited about the psychiatric possibilities of LSD. He had been in psychoanalysis in the past and thought that a single trip with LSD was as good as a thousand sessions with a psychiatrist, in terms of the self-knowledge that it generated. Most people reporting the insight gained on their trips are vague and mystical, but David's knowledge about himself was precise and was similar to the more or less ordinary insights gained from conventional psychotherapy. He became aware of his mother's negative attitudes towards men and especially towards his father and was able to relate those attitudes to his own recurrent colitis. There is a real possibility that on his trip he merely remembered with emotional force something that his psychiatrist had told him years ago and that he had forgotten.

David was in the process of writing the third and final part of a book on the drug experience; that part would deal with LSD and mystical, especially ESP, experiences. He had already been interested in all sorts of ESP, especially thought-transference, and felt that people under LSD were sensitive enough and closely enough attuned to each other that emotions, visions, and ideas could flow non-verbally from person to person. He described two friends of his who had been on a trip in Tompkins Square Park and who were seeing creeping, crawling things. When either one of the two saw a creepy-crawler, the other one simultaneously saw the same thing and at the same place. His own experience had been simpler but more interesting: He had put his hand on his girl friend's hand when she was painting and had really felt the energy flowing through her hand as it moved, and had been aware of the intensity of that energy and of its status as part of the cosmic energy that flows through everything.

David thinks that after several more trips he'll have cleared up all his problems and be a happy person. The drug has already made him decide that he wants to be a painter rather than a writer, even though he will finish his book on drugs. He wants to paint like Jackson Pollock, using his whole body, perhaps tacking up huge canvasses and then running back and forth with a roller, expressing his unconscious with immense swirls and blobs of paint.

Somehow, on the second meeting, David seemed less vivid, less articulate, even less sophisticated than he had on the first meeting. It was, for example, naive of him to want to emulate Jackson Pollock, a great-enough painter but one who has already made the particular statement that can be made by that style of painting. It seemed, too, that drugs had turned him further and further away from contact with the outside world. He told us, for example, about being on a trip and seeing a nurse going home from work who was frightened of him. He didn't understand why at first, and then realized that he was on a trip and was acting peculiarly. It is, he says, harder and harder to realize that some other people haven't been on trips, and he has great difficulty communicating with members of straight society. But while he feels that his inability to communicate with straight society is one of the hang-ups which he hopes repeated LSD trips will help him over, there is a greater likelihood that repeated trips will make his communication with the rest of us more and more difficult.

David made us aware, too, of some of the unpleasant aspects of the drug. He showed us a seventeen-year-old girl with whom he had just been talking. She was a fairly attractive girl, with long tangled blond hair, who walked as though in a happy daze. She exists, David said, almost permanently turned on, with no money and no place to stay, but somehow she manages to eat and to get lodging. Apparently she comes from a fairly wealthy family and does call them for money occasionally. I saw her in Tompkins Square Park later that day and on succeeding occasions. She was always walking in the vague, distracted way that people have when they are turned on, sometimes alone, usually with a young man, never the same one twice.

There is another young man in the park who is, as David puts it, not yet down from a trip that he had begun with twenty thousand micrograms of LSD two months earlier (the ordinary amount is two hundred and fifty micrograms). He, too, wanders about with a permanent happy smile on his face. So far as I know nobody has tried to give either of these kids any serious help for what may already be, or may turn into, permanent schizophrenia.

There is a group of devotees that meets in Tompkins Square Park every Sunday afternoon and chants for a couple of hours the names of the Buddhist gods whom they worship. They burn incense, and sway in a semi-mystical trance as they chant. During one of these meetings I had noticed two young blonds, not terribly pretty, seventeen and nineteen years old. The older one seemed to be one of the most ecstatic of the chanters. The same evening, I saw her being interviewed on a television news program where she said that she was a hippie because her father had been a beatnik. There just hadn't been enough time for beatniks to have grown-up hippie children, and so the next time I saw her in the park I asked her about that and about herself in general. She said that her father, now dead, had been a junky in San Francisco's North Beach during the forties. She struck me throughout our conversation as an extremely intelligent and talented girl. At the time I talked to her, she was finishing a dress for herself, and she said that she made part of the money she needed to live on by working as a seamstress and part by working in the Psychedelicatessen, a shop described later in this study.

She had been, under her father's influence, an early and voracious reader, and had left college after the first year mostly because there was no challenge in it for her. The English teacher, especially, had assigned books she had read when she was much younger, and, according to her, the teacher knew less about them than she did. She said that she still read a lot, naming as her present favorites Aldous Huxley, William Faulkner, J. R. R. Tolkien, and Bob Dylan. She also had been a civil rights activist, working in the South with SNCC, going on a freedom ride from Birmingham to Washington, and finally dropping out of civil rights because she saw the futility of it all.

As for religion, her mother was a member of the Jehovah's Witnesses and her father had been a Catholic. She could not take the dogma and rigidity of either religion, but in the Catholic church she had found that the incense, the music, and the stained glass offered the same kind of total environment that the psychedelic generation values so much. She loved the Jehovah's Witnesses as people. She would seriously like to go back to a meeting of the Jehovah's Witnesses and put LSD in the punch to turn them all on because "they're all such beautiful people and deserve to be turned on." The fact is that the religious impulse is still strong in her. When she was a little girl, she said, she wanted to write a book that would save the whole world, and even now she thinks in terms of a world that needs to be saved, though the agent now would not be a book but LSD.

She is one of the heaviest users of LSD that I talked to. She was currently taking about one thousand micrograms twice a week, though earlier, on the coast, she had been taking it each day. For her, a trip is "like you're in a special place. A glass bubble. Nothing bad can happen to you when you're tripping." She said that all her senses were working at once, and that all of the senses worked along with thought, with knowing. When she was on a trip she perceived colors in terms of words and shadows and hearing and feeling. If a record was playing, it communicated to her thought waves from whoever was singing or playing or perhaps even from the author or composer.

The other girl was her sister. While we were talking, she had been sprinkling sand in minute quantities around the base of a tree and in a large cavity about four feet up the trunk, murmuring a spell. Occasionally the older girl got up to help her. They told me that they were working witchcraft but that it wasn't going to hurt anybody, not even the tree. The sand was magical sand, a mixture of sand from holy places like the backyards of Bob Dylan and Timothy Leary. They wouldn't tell me what the spell was supposed to accomplish because if they told it wouldn't work. But previous spells had worked, and the subject of the spell seemed on the whole to be boys. After all, they were teen-age girls.

In New York, the two had been living with a group of

about ten boys who were now in California, but they were soon leaving to join the boys out West. The older girl felt that she had no psycho-sexual hang-ups, but that a number of hippie girls still thought they were surrendering something when they made love with a man. (That, presumably, was her definition of a sexual hang-up.)

Because so many hippies are of college age and have, in fact, been to college, the summer hippie is a common enough phenomenon. The summer hippie appears on the scene about the time that school lets out, and he doesn't really know whether or not he'll return to school in the fall. He does know that he'll go back sometime, somewhere, but he is imprecise about where or when. There is no reason to say that summer hippies are not hippies because they share in all manifestations of hippie existence — the drugs, the free love, the voluntary poverty, the urge to self-fulfillment — and they all indicate that in some way or another they have made permanent changes in their life styles, even if they do return to work or study in the straight world. In a way, the summer hippie may turn out to be one of the most influential members of the hippie community, for if he moves back into the world of straight society while keeping his hippie values he may do a lot to leaven (or taint or corrupt, depending on your point of view) the society in which he lives.

I met one typical summer hippie in Tompkins Square Park on a warm evening in July. She was wearing a beige, tailored blouse (or perhaps it was simply a man's shirt), jeans torn off slightly above the knee, a bandanna around her head like an Indian headband, and a button that said "Protect the Grass" (a rather weak pun based on *grass* as one of the names for marijuana). When I first saw her she was sitting on a park bench, and then went over to sit on the real grass under a tree. She looked lonely and so I didn't mind talking to her because I figured that she would be happy to talk to somebody. She was.

She was a fairly attractive girl, but would have passed on first glance in any college as ordinary, perhaps even a bit more straitlaced than average. Her college was a Midwestern state school where she was majoring in psychology, hoping to become a child psychologist. She had no particular plans about marriage but presumed that she would marry, and while she didn't explicitly plan to stay a hippie for the rest of her life she said that she would never accept a life in which she couldn't occasionally sit under a tree, or go out and buy an ice-cream cone or a balloon, or fly a kite if she wanted to. In a sense, the hippie life for her was the freedom to be like a child.

She had taken three trips on LSD, and knew that the first trip was on a dose of two hundred and fifty micrograms, but did not know the dosage of the other two. The major thing on her first — and apparently most significant — trip had been that she and the two other people she took it with had sat around talking about love. Her attitudes towards love were simple. Basically, for her, one showed love to somebody when he could make the other person feel that he was a really important and unique human being. In sex and marriage the only good relationship for her was one of sharing, sharing not only joy but sorrow and sadness, a simple relationship of complete give-and-take. She disapproved of much of the promiscuous love that went on in the East Village on the part of girls who somehow thought that they should sleep with anybody who wanted them to, and who ended up sleeping with different men each night. (This was, however, a pattern that I suspect is relatively rare, except, perhaps, among members of settled communities.) She felt that one should sleep with a person only when one knows, understands, and likes him.

Her relationship with her parents was warm and grateful. She thought that this was true of most of the people she knew in the East Village, although she admitted that she had an unusually good relationship with her parents because they knew and approved of where she was and what, in general, she was doing. They did not, however, know that she was using marijuana or LSD, but she thought that she would eventually tell them when she went back home. I asked her if she wanted to turn her parents on (that is, convince them to take an LSD trip). She thought a long time and finally said, "Yes, I think I'd like to share with them my experiences."

As we talked longer, however, her relationship with her parents began to show more complexity. At first, she had expressed conventional gratitude because they had provided her with education and introduced her to art, literature, music, and the theater. But she later indicated that she thought of her parents as having been tied down with children and responsibilities and paying the bills, and that very likely they regretted a number of opportunities that they had missed in their youth. This, of course, is far from "Daddy works hard for you in an office all day and Mommy works her fingers to the bone," but the spirit is similar.

Because she looked not only lonely but bored when I decided to talk to her, I asked her if she didn't often feel bored just hanging around, and she was incredulous that I should even have asked. There was no boredom in the East Village, she said; she read or wrote or sat under a tree.

She had not grown up in a church, but when she was fourteen she and her parents began going to a Unitarian church. Perhaps this rather bland early religious experience accounted for her not really seeing the LSD experience as anything specifically religious. She learned a little more about what was in her, the way she thought and felt about things, but there was no "great big revelation."

Unlike most hippies, she believed in political activism. She had worked with the Student Nonviolent Coordinating Committee (SNCC), had marched in protest demonstrations, picketed, and even gotten newspaper publicity for all of this. And she would continue as an activist. As she put it, "Whether we like it or not, we live in a real world, with real people, and real problems — those are real children being killed in Vietnam, and that's real blood being spilled over there."

GALAHAD'S COMMUNE

Even in the West Village I had heard about Galahad's Commune which was located just a few blocks from Tompkins Square Park. Part of my interest in the commune came from a story on it that appeared in the *New York Times* the day after the 1967 Memorial Day riots in the park. For some reason the *Times* called it a Digger Commune and said that as many as fifteen "Diggers" a night stay there, but its similarity to the San Francisco Diggers is not great. (The *New York Times* also defined "Digger" as a hippie with no noticeable income, which is

40

inaccurate. The Digger movement in San Francisco is a loose but fairly well-defined group that has modeled itself on a seventeenth-century movement of English farmers.)

The commune is organized and supervised by a twenty-one-year-old boy from Kansas City who is known as Galahad, for no particularly good reason. The theory behind the commune is simply that anyone who needs free food and lodging may get it, though of a Spartan and not overly clean sort. Theoretically, drugs of any sort are not allowed in the commune for the rather simple reason that the police are suspicious of it and would be happy enough to find a reason to close it down. The major problem of the commune seems to be the number of suburban runaways who wander in and, because of the free sexual life of the inhabitants, are likely to get somebody in trouble for impairing the morals of minors. Galahad himself was arrested on such a charge, probably unjustly. Galahad tries to discourage runaways and takes them back to their homes where he talks to the child and the parent about what went wrong. According to the *Times:*

> One such parent, Mrs. Selma Donnelly, the mother of a 13-year-old boy from Queens, came to the commune Saturday night with Galahad's wallet, which he had left at her home when he took her son home. She put $5 in it "because you paid for the carfare to get him home."
> "Thanks for my wallet," Galahad said.
> "Thanks for my son," Mrs. Donnelly replied.*

Other parents have given a television set and a radio to the commune.

One of the most attractive features of Galahad and the commune is their attitude towards the police. The day

* *New York Times,* June 1, 1967, p. 45.

after Galahad's arrest he and a group of the residents showed up at the police station carrying buckets of paint and offered to paint the walls of the station because they had noticed that they were dirty. Earlier, when they offered to wash the police cars belonging to the precinct, the police, according to Galahad, "told me to shut-the-hell-up."

Galahad told the *Times* reporter that he had been raised in the church and still believed strongly in God and that God is the answer to the problems of the world. The last time I saw Galahad, he was standing on the sidewalk in front of the Psychedelicatessen shooting a water pistol at a policeman who was pretending not to notice.

I first visited the commune on a warm Sunday afternoon about three weeks after the story had been written. I carried a large bag of apples with me, and they were immediately accepted, not for any common food supply as I had imagined, but as individual treats by the young people standing talking in the hallway. The kids are, in fact, beggars, so that when I go there I always carry an extra pack of cigarettes and a pocketful of change. But that particular afternoon they made me extremely aware that if they were exploiting me, they knew that I was exploiting them. One photographer from a national magazine had arrived with a letter from Allen Ginsberg — a naive idea because most of the kids there have never even heard of Allen Ginsberg. The photographer met with a fierce reception. Several of the kids felt that if he was going to take pictures, as if they were animals in a zoo, and then make money selling the pictures, he at least ought to pay them something for the upkeep of the commune. He didn't have cigarettes to hand out, nor did he stop and talk to them as if they were people. He just wanted to take pictures, and I was sympathetic with the kids even though I expected to be evicted next. Ultimately, the photographer left.

Most of my conversation was with the leader of the insurrection against the photographer, a young Negro called Preacher, who said that he'd trust me only if I gave him seventy-five cents to buy a bottle of wine and then share the wine with him. The challenge was an interesting one and I admired him for it. First he got the wine, which was terrible stuff, free. Then he could test not only my generosity but — and most important — my willingness to drink from a bottle that a *black hippie* had just drunk from. Whether he was aware that it was also a kind of crude sacramental gesture that established a communion between us, I don't know.

So far, I've probably made Preacher sound cheap; but he actually was bright and extremely commune-oriented. He really *believed* in the commune, in the ideals of sharing, and in the kind of life that they lived there. In fact he was trying to get enough interest aroused to begin a commune somewhere else because that one was getting crowded. And, in all fairness, I have never gone into this building near Tompkins Square Park without being offered food and a corner of a mattress.

Most of the kids were sitting around in a room on the third floor of the building, talking, reading, or playing cards. There was a dirty sink in the corner, mattresses were piled all over, and there was almost no other furniture. After the reporter had left, two boys, one white and one black, emerged from the group like an explosion, slugging with all the frustrated, welled-up hatred that a human being can hold. The black boy, whom I talked to some time later, had a cast on his arm and was using it with bloody effect on the white boy, a hard-looking Southerner wearing a black leather jacket. I tried to get between them but Preacher jumped on me and pulled me back. He said that I could have been killed, and I suspect he was right. Later, when I left, I talked outside to the white boy, who was still burning with hatred. He vowed that he was going to kill the other boy and would do it that very evening. He invited me to stay around for the story. I asked him what had become of all the talk of love that I heard up there and throughout the East Village. "That's okay," he said. "I love everybody — even Al — but I'm going to kill that black bastard this evening." I said that I hoped he wouldn't stay violent, that he would learn to live up to his own ideals. "Too bad about that," he mumbled.

After the fight, the talk settled down to what sounded as if it might have been a constant topic of discussion — the operation of the commune. Preacher had already told me that the real problem of the commune was the number of people who contributed nothing, no food, no work, no money, but just stayed to live free. The group was talking about whether there was any need for rules and regulations. It was poignant. Like all hippies, they had dropped out of organized society partly in protest against anything like system and organization; now they were faced with the concrete fact of filth and squalor just because they had no organization of their own.

They also complained about Galahad, the folk hero of the *New York Times*. Preacher particularly felt that Galahad had taken to staying by himself in his own room and visiting the other rooms of the commune only to hand down orders. One girl complained that just

44

that morning Galahad had said, "Let's go clean up the roof." (A lot of commune activity seems to go on up on the roof, a normal practice in New York.) But, she said, when they got up on the roof and started working, they discovered that Galahad wasn't there. He had, in fact, behaved like the boy scout leader who says, "Now, boys, let's clean up the area," before he sits down on a stump.

From the fight and the nature of the talk, it was clear that the commune had about run its course.

The next time I visited the commune it was late at night, after I had more or less intentionally missed my bus back to New Jersey. Some of the people who had been there when I visited it earlier recognized me and assured the rest that I was straight but okay. In fact, suspicion was so well removed that I saw what I assume were drugs — probably amphetamines or methedone, but not likely LSD — handed around freely. That night I was offered a place to sleep, but it was clear the kids preferred to talk.

Sex dominated the conversation that evening, but it was not the calm, accepting kind of sex that one assumes is part of their program of free love — it was tense and tearful. Shortly after I got there, one of the boys, carrying his banjo and a bag of clothes, started out the door — at 2:00 A.M. — to go to San Francisco, because he had had some trouble with his girl friend. Several others tried to persuade him to stay, but he was adamant. (He returned about two hours later, and rather sheepishly slunk by us, back up to his girl.)

Most of the time I spent talking to a good-looking redhead named Angel, whose problems were right out on the surface for anybody to see. He had been having

45

some kind of trouble with his girl friend, too, and she was not taking his consolation but had to talk it out, weeping, with John, Angel's best friend.

Angel was having general problems with the whole idea of love. He knew that he should love but found it hard to. Furthermore, he felt that his aggressiveness was just about out of control, claiming that he had already killed two people and that he could kill me and then get a good night's sleep. For him, drugs were simply a high, a kick, and I got the impression that he took just about anything that he could find. I tried to tell him that underneath he was a warm, soft person who had probably been hurt — that his toughness was a mask, and not a very convincing mask at that. But just before I left, another girl came running down, crying that somebody had almost raped her and then run away across the roofs. It had been one of the Negroes that lived in the building. The girl was John's girl, and Angel became furious, vowing that he would kill the boy. It was as simple as that, he said, the boy was going to be dead and that's all there would be to it. Angel really looked and talked like a killer. Both times, then, that I visited the house, my last moments had been with somebody who was vowing to kill somebody else. There are, definitely, thorns on the stems of the flower children of New York.

More recent events have only elongated these thorns — at least in the eyes of the nation. A recent and devastatingly tragic double murder on New York's Lower East Side claimed as one of its victims one "Groovy" Hutchinson, a young hippie who has been identified as a sometime resident of Galahad's. Arrests have since been made in the case — and it is important to point out that those accused of committing the crime do not belong to the hippie generation.

My last visit to the building was made with my wife. We met Angel shortly after we got in the door, and he had, in about a week, undergone something like a conversion experience under the influence of LSD. He finally understood himself, he said, and knew that deep down he was able to love and forgive. He was at peace with himself and ready to love and forgive anybody, no matter what the other person had done. He invited us to his room in the building but warned us that it would be strange because everybody except him was on a trip and he was watching over the whole bunch. Just as we walked in the door, Cheryl, a little Negro girl sitting on a couch fondling a kitten, said, "Who are these lovely people?" That set the tone for the evening. Cheryl had come from California with her boyfriend Lucky, about whom she wanted to talk because she was terribly proud of him and of being his. They came on freight cars as far as Indiana where the railroad detectives threw them off, and they hitchhiked the rest of the way to New York. Cheryl was one of the most charming people I met down there, at least when she was turned on.

Soon, though, I began talking to George, a college boy with a guitar over his shoulder, who talked to me non-stop for about an hour. (I think that he was high on amphetamine, which is an energizer.) First he told me about a girl he had met there the previous day, whom he had taken a liking to. He had asked her to travel with him across the United States by way of New Orleans by boxcar and hitchhiking and she had agreed to go after a moment's thought. They were leaving in a couple of days. He was thrilled to find a girl like that, who would just take off across the country with a man she had just met.

George was one of those sophomoric philosophers I have always found attractive, who pick up an abstract idea and chew it to bits. His idea was that man was essentially wicked and selfish. His reasoning was naive enough: he reasoned that all men are born into a situation in which they immediately begin to selfishly gratify themselves at their mother's breasts and that forms their basic character for the rest of their lives. He told me a number of stories about the essential meanness of men, including one experience that filled him with the most indignation. That was when he had joined a group of "Bughouse Square" bums in Chicago to get a free meal at a mission. First he had to attend a religious service; then, if he wanted a meal, he had to say that he accepted the Lord Jesus Christ as his Savior. He was hungry and so he did. But as though that wasn't bad enough, he had to talk to a "counselor," who asked him again whether he was saved and when. He told the counselor that he had always been a Christian; but when the counselor marked his record card, George noticed that he checked "new conversion."

If George's concerns, then, were sophomoric, they revealed a great deal about George. First, he still had enough of conventional religious sentiment to have been deeply disillusioned and angered by the shoddiness of any aspect of society representing Christianity; and second, his idea that all men are essentially evil was in direct opposition to the hippies' whole working set of assumptions, which are that all men are essentially kind and loving if only they are left alone to be themselves and to do their own things. I think that George really

48

wanted me to tell him that his idea wasn't so, because he was a boy who wanted a faith of some sort, and at the time I talked to him he had faith only in a chick who was willing to take her chances with him hitchhiking across America.

I told George about the aggressiveness that I'd seen earlier in the house and he said that San Francisco was the same way, that out there they talk even more than in New York about peace and love, but that they are just as aggressive and likely to fight as in New York.

George also had a poem that he recited for me — he had no copies but had memorized it. It was a series of images of San Francisco and the psychedelic life, and it included a series of questions asking what, if anything, it all meant. He was clearly making a learning experience out of his hippie days, and he had learned a lot that isn't learned in schools. When he had arrived in San Francisco some months earlier, looking like a hippie and accompanied by a fifteen-year-old girl he had met just on the edge of town, he was immediately picked up for impairing the morals of a minor. He was taken into the police station where he said he saw police brutality firsthand. At the time he had been on an LSD trip, and he began thinking about how clever it would be to escape from the police. So he did, running out the door of the station and into nearby Golden Gate Park where he hid in bushes until the police decided that he wasn't there.

Al talked mostly to my wife. He had been the Negro in the fight that had taken place when I was there before, but now the cast was off his arm and he was warm and gentle. He was not on a trip of any sort; in fact, he had taken LSD twice and felt that he had gotten from

49

the drug so much self-understanding that he would never need to take another trip. Surprisingly, what he seemed to have learned was that one should not be ruled by one's emotions but by the intellect, the most anomalous of the attitudes that I had seen emerging from the LSD experience. But the strangest thing about his last LSD trip was that while on it he had begun to feel intense pains in the palms of his hands, pains that kept getting worse and worse, "almost," he said, "as though somebody was driving nails into them." The possibility of an LSD-stimulated stigmata is real, if vaguely disturbing.

Eventually we went to Al's apartment, where his roommate was sleeping on the floor. The rooms were clean and neat though barely furnished — it had mattresses instead of beds, for example. Al played Indian music for us on his record player and talked about memories. Memories must be forgotten, he felt, or at least controlled; otherwise, they would control you.

Before we left, we went back to say good-bye to Angel. When we walked in, he motioned us back because he had some business that had to go on in quiet. Another boy, a young, handsome blond youth, had been offended by a straight on the street and was in a killing mood. He was sitting in a chair with Angel leaning over him, his arms on the chair arms, haranguing like a Southern Baptist minister: "You've got to learn to *love* and *forgive*, man. That's *all*. You've just got to learn to *forgive*, because hating ain't hurting *nobody* but *yourself*. Now you *can* forgive, you *really can;* just *think* about it, think *real hard* about it; think about what's *really important*. Now I want you just to go over there and sit and *think* about what I told you." And the boy did, in fact, go over to a corner and sit and think, hard.

50

The rooms, except for Al's, were dirty. There were roaches on the floor and dirty pots and pans on the windowsill; and everybody drank out of a common glass in the sink. The hallway stank, and there were little piles of garbage in the corners. But there was a moving atmosphere of warmth and acceptance in the whole building that evening. Everything was gentleness, soft-spokenness, even love. Because they offered food and lodging — still — to anybody who came in, they opened themselves to invasion by nosey straights such as we; but since all we wanted to do was talk, they talked freely and openly, without defensiveness, self-consciousness, resentment, or even condescension to straight society.

HIPPIE ENTREPRENEURS

Many hippies work, of course, some because they have to sustain themselves, some at jobs they find personally fulfilling. But I was curious about the phenomenon of the hippie shopkeeper because the older Bohemian, or even beatnik, tradition had seemed "anti" anything so conventional as keeping a shop. I think I suspected that the shopkeepers weren't really hippies but just smart entrepreneurs who thought they knew a good thing when they saw it and were setting up for the rush of tourists over the summer. I decided to talk to a number of the owners of the gaudy shops scattered throughout the area.

The Sanctuary Coffee House is in a basement on Eighth Street between First and Second Avenues. There were about seven circular signs in the window, all saying "God Save the Stones" — a reference to the recent

arrest of Mick Jagger, a member of the Rolling Stones.*
The shop, set up with about five small plywood booths
along one wall, was empty when I went in except for
the young man who was managing it. He had just
opened it for the evening and nothing was ready — he
had begun heating water in two pyrex pots to make
the coffee. Unlike the older, established coffeehouses,
there was no impressive espresso machine, no fancy, expensive coffees. They had tea — black, Lipton's, and with
lemon — for twenty-five cents, and coffee, mostly just
American coffee, for thirty-five cents. The menu also
listed potato chips and doughnuts. As much as anything
else, the operation had the air of a children's lemonade
stand on a suburban sidewalk in the summer.

The young man in charge of the place was not the
owner. The owner had started it but decided that he
didn't enjoy running it, and he was back at school,
probably studying either computer design or English
literature. The manager himself was a student at the
University of Virginia, interested mainly in the technical aspects of the drama, and was with a small drama
group just getting underway in the East Village. He
had a great deal of bushy black hair and a young beard,
and he was wearing a button that said simply "Trotsky."

---

* Mick had been arrested at a party where he was found to
have in his pocket four tablets of a drug in the dexedrine group
(for pepping up and preventing nausea). It was a drug ordinarily sold by prescription in England. But Mick had gotten
the tablets in Italy and had brought them into England, thus
technically committing a crime even though he had discussed
the pills with his own physician and the physician had thought
that they would be all right for him to take. The signs in the
coffeehouse window, then, were a combination of an expression
of the centrality of music to hippies and an objection to society's
repressive tactics.

I asked about the Trotsky button and he was just a bit vague about why he was wearing it, except that he knew he looked somewhat like Trotsky and he had been associated with a Trotskyite group. In general, he was, he said, wearing it for "personal" reasons.

The coffeehouse paid the rent. It was not a money-making venture, and customers were few, usually the same people who wandered in evening after evening to talk. That, of course, was the secret of why the young man was there at all. He liked to talk to people and in a coffeehouse he could. My questions to him tended to be blundering. I asked him if he liked the life in the East Village, and he said that it wasn't really something that you liked or didn't like. You just lived it. Nor was he looking for excitement. All he really wanted was to be somewhere where he wasn't, well, vegetating.

The Psychedelicatessen is the center of the East Side hippie existence. It's only a few doors away from Tompkins Square Park, near the Something (a restaurant), the Cave (a coffee shop), and a leather-goods store. Since all these businesses are hippie-oriented, they together form something like a hippie shopping center. The importance to the area of the Psychedelicatessen is manifest by the notices on the wall just inside the door, notices offering and asking for rides to Chicago, San Francisco, Millbrook; notices offering to share apartments or asking for apartments; notices asking for "an understanding chick" who would live and love with a "sensitive, alert, young man" for a couple of months before school started in the fall. And finally, there were always a couple of pathetic notices begging somebody or another to come or call home because "we love you and need you" and signed "Mom and Dad."

The Psychedelicatessen sells posters, paintings, candles, magazines and newspapers of the underground press (it was, for example, the only place where I saw *Inner Space* and the *Psychedelic Review* for sale), jewelry, especially earrings, beads, pendants, and bells. It's a marvellous and exciting place to browse in and it was set up precisely for that. Whenever I went in, people were wandering through, mostly browsing but often buying. And almost all of the browsers and buyers were hippies themselves. The two young men at the counter told me that most of their trade is from hippies and that though they don't resent the tourists — people from "uptown" ("uptown" is, of course, a state of mind that includes far downtown, Long Island, Westchester, and Connecticut as well) — the tourists are the ones who do most of the shoplifting. This includes the college students, who come to stare superciliously, and, unavoidably, heroin addicts, who steal everywhere, all the time.

The Psychedelicatessen had been open for only six months and was, when I visited it, in debt for nine hundred dollars. But the debt resulted from a couple of characteristic factors. First, when it opened, they had served free food in the shop, about forty dollars' worth a day. This was not only expensive but also tended to discourage trade because people did not ordinarily want to go into a shop to browse or buy when a group was sitting around eating; it would be like buying in somebody's dining room. Still, the young man I talked to regretted that they couldn't go on serving food to people. The other reason is that the shop employs a total of sixteen people. (It stays open extremely late at night, but I would find it hard to imagine that more than three people were necessary to keep it going.) It employs these people because the owners want to help the members of the community. Still the Psychedelicatessen sells its goods for prices lower than those of most of the other shops in the area and is popular because of that. It may well make it and become a permanent part of the East Village scene. The men I talked to estimated that if it lasted through the following winter, when business would be slow, it would survive.

One of the items they sell a great deal of is cigarette paper, several boxes of which were ranged on the counter in front of the cash register. These, of course, were used for rolling marijuana cigarettes. The men in the store say that a college student or other tourist will occasionally glide up and whisper, "Can you give me some pot?" — no doubt on the assumption that such stores are really fronts for the sale of marijuana or perhaps even LSD. Even the police keep a check on the store for pretty much the same reason. The fact is, of course, that such shops are too much fun and too useful to the community to endanger themselves by selling anything illegal — unless, of course, some of the magazines are declared illegal.

One of the young men in the shop was planning to go back to school at CCNY in the fall and simultaneously open his own shop, to sell the various literary and psychedelic publications that are proliferating so fast that no one shop can keep up with them now. When I asked about the apparent anomaly of hippie merchants their reply was quite simple: "Look, in the city you can't grow your own food or make your own clothes from leather or bark or something. You've got to have money to live on. So different people do different things. We have a shop." But I suspect that even if they didn't need the money to live on they would still run the shop, still employ sixteen people, and perhaps be able to continue serving food.

Slightly west of the rest of the East Village itself is one of the larger and more established shops, Elephants Are Contagious. Many of the items that they sell are part of the commercially produced material cashing in on the current interest in the psychedelic life — there is even a set of stacking cards called LSD, commercially produced and boxed, for suburban children to get vicarious non-chemical kicks. There is a commercially produced set of skin decals, called Tatu, sold there. But they also sell wide neckties, rag dolls, painted candlesticks, jewelry, cups, and bells, most of which have been crafted by local people. This shop does, so far as I can tell, get a good bit of tourist trade, and though it is a good browsing shop it was less exciting — perhaps because of the commercially produced stuff — than the Psychedelicatessen. It reminded me somewhat of the artsy-craftsy tourist shops near resort areas in the White Mountains. I suspect that in a year or two they will be selling pencils and ashtrays with a picture of a couple of hippies and "Souvenir of the East Village" written on them.

Elephants Are Contagious is owned by three people. One of the owners, a polite, slender young man with a slight accent that I couldn't place, was working at the time I went in, assisted somewhat by his wife who was sitting behind the counter feeding a one-year-old child. They were suspicious of the whole concept of hippie, and said that they did most of their selling to "tourist hippies" — roughly equivalent to weekend hippies. The fact is, of course, that few hippies have enough money to spend on shopping for anything besides food, shelter, and drugs. I asked the man if he considered himself a hippie, and his wife said, "What a question to ask!" I agreed, of course, but I had found a number of people who were proud enough to say Yes. The man did say, finally, that in certain company and at certain times they might call themselves hippies.

The Paranoia is a tiny shop that occupies the street room of a four-room flat. It is owned by three girls, one a fourth-grade teacher in Harlem, one a cartoonist, and one a computer programmer. They sell much the same sort of things that the other psychedelic shops sell except that, with few exceptions, their merchandise is all made by local artists who give them their goods on consignment. They have an especially good assortment of handmade cards and collage paintings. Financially, they are about two thousand dollars in debt after about two months' operation. The first month they grossed four hundred dollars. That is why they laughed when I asked them if they saw any anomaly in hippies being merchants. In a sense, it might be possible to say that the girls work in order to support the shop which they love and which gives them a place in life that provides them with emotional reward and meaning.

The teacher was in the shop when I went in. When I told her what I was doing she thought it was a marvelous idea because she, like the hippies in the park, desperately wanted her way of life explained. She offered me stew, and she did have, indeed, a huge kettle of stew in the kitchen just behind the shop. Her offer was made pretty much as a matter of course because the girls make a practice of offering free stew to anybody who wants it during dinnertime. Usually hippies who are broke or neighborhood children come in to eat the stew. (The free food is certainly not a come-on for potential customers, because potential customers don't need free meals.)

In back of the kitchen is the "trip room." This is a small room with brightly painted figures on the walls and ceiling, and a simulated T.V. set in the corner with bright moving lines on it. The paint used is the kind of iridescent paint that glows brightly in ultra-violet light, and the room was permanently lighted by ultra-violet lamps. I don't know whether the room is actually used for LSD trips or whether it only simulates the effect of an LSD trip. She explained, simply, that the children liked the room. Behind the "trip room" was the "meditation room," which was more subdued, with what looked like Far Eastern motifs painted on the walls. On that day, the children were there, sitting around listening to music on a record player. My guide made all of the children introduce themselves to me — showing her public-school orientation — and explained that they were simply neighborhood children who like to gather in there and who eat the free food every evening. Ordinarily, though, the meditation room was used for hippies who came in off the street during the day and wanted to get away from the noise and general confusion of the city.

She was proud to be called a hippie and was proud of the setup that they had there. If they got too far in debt, they would simply fold up, having enjoyed the experience immensely. Unfortunately, they too had trouble from "uptown," which included, besides the shoplifters, the landlord, who had had the bad grace to inform them in writing that he didn't like hippies and that he wanted them to move. If they ever do move, he'll have for rent one of the most interestingly decorated shops in New York.

THE HIPPIE STYLE

Hippie Dress

Most suburbanites, when fishing, working in their yards, or just loafing on vacation, tend to wear the distinctive clothing of the working class. This clothing includes comfortable work shirts, denim or khaki trousers, old shoes or sneakers (or they may go barefoot). They also tend not to shave nor to be fastidious about getting haircuts. That sort of thing is, in general, what characterizes hippie dress — old clothes and often bare feet. Whatever is distinctive about hippie dress and appearance is the result of not taking the trouble more than the result of putting on some specific costume. Even a number of teeny-boppers are beginning to dress in this way rather than in the more expensive and distinctive mod clothes. Not taking the trouble is also the source of the generally shabby appearance of hippies. It is not usually that their clothes are dirty but that they have at most only two sets of clothing, so that what they have wears out quickly.

Hippies do, on the other hand, tend to decorate themselves like primitive people, with earrings, beads, and bells. Some wear "tattoos," either painted on or put on with decals. A few wear Indian headbands, and occasionally one wears something that looks more like a robe than Western dress.

Hippie Economy

The hippie economy is, quite simply, voluntary poverty. Most hippies have seen their parents work and struggle for material goods and miss anything like meaning in life; thus they deduce that the way to happiness and self-fulfillment through increasing one's material goods is a futile way, and they determine instead to live life not in terms of what they have but in terms of what they can do without. Hence, their apartments are sparsely furnished — beds are not necessary though mattresses are; chairs and tables can be kept to a minimum or even eliminated. Their food is simple and inexpensive. Many learn to beg leftover food from restaurants or even to pick over garbage cans, though the last is rare in New York anyway. An example of hippie economy is found in a letter in the *East Village Other:*

> Till our second baby arrived I could feed three on about $15 per week, and hippies on less than $1 a day could provide themselves with the basic food needs. It's summer so you don't need much. Oatmeal, if taken with a sprinkling of salt, is a real meal and you can get about 20 portions from the 27¢ box. . . . Give up sodas — 30¢ will buy six eggs. One quick meal with no cooking is — yolk of one or two eggs beaten or shaken to a slight froth, add more or less milk, a little sugar to taste, a drop or two of vanilla essence for extra taste. . . . Buy oranges instead of orange juice. You don't need a whole orange to keep scurvy away. . . .

And so forth for about a thousand words of advice on saving money in washing clothes, eating, and housing. The chances are that the writer of the letter had a couple of years of college, as did her husband, and that their parents probably average a combined total of about forty thousand dollars annually because the letter has a thoroughly prudent, middle-class ring to it. The only thing not middle class about it, in fact, is that she and her husband have chosen to live a life of poverty to avoid what they see as the spiritual deformity that results from attempts to make a lot of money.

Many hippies do work, and in New York City they have no trouble finding jobs since they are young, capable, and for the most part have some college experience. But they will not do work that they find meaningless, or if they do, they will keep a job only long enough to live for a while on their savings. Some also get allowances from their parents. Many live communally, that is, six to twelve in an apartment, sharing the work and the money and thus living much more cheaply than they could living two or three in an apartment.

The difference between voluntary poverty and plain poverty is, however, immense, and the difference doesn't lie altogether in the realm of the spirit, for voluntary poverty does depend on the consciousness that one can leave it at any time one wants. Thus most hippies know that they *could* get a full-time job and keep it; they *could* go back to college; they *could*, presumably, even go back to the suburbs to live with parents. Also, the existence of suburban parents gives the hippies a kind of security that a simply poor person does not have. If, for example, a hippie or his children needed expensive medical care, it would be furnished. If he needed bail money to get out of jail, that would be furnished. The suburban parents can even take over the expense of sending grandchildren to college, if the hippie phenomenon lasts long enough.

This aspect of voluntary poverty is what makes the Negro hippie a phenomenon that some Negro observers deplore. For unless the Negro hippie is one of those rare Negroes with families who have made it financially he is on an equal with his white friends only until they need extra money or decide to go back to straight society. And even when an eviction notice comes from the landlord, the white hippie can often send home for extra money, while the Negro hippie has to go out on the streets — with much less chance of finding another apartment than the white hippie.

All of this does not necessarily mean that voluntary poverty is phony any more than it is phony for a suburban family to go camping, or to drive to a hiking trail and hike up a mountain when they could very well have driven up the mountain, or for a middle-class banker to go fishing when he could get his fish at a nearby fish market. Voluntary poverty may be a temporary style for many, but it does represent a cast of mind that may well remain for the rest of the hippie's life; for once a man has learned what he can do without he attains real freedom from onerous, meaningless work, carried on for the sake of status, for excessive security, or for luxuries that do not provide real human self-fulfillment. He is more free to be human, no matter what his income level happens to be.

Sex

Hippies practice free love. This is not often written about them, but the hippies themselves, of both sexes, are quite open and unembarrassed about it. In fact, they aren't even terribly proud of it nor are they coy when when they discuss it, since it is such a normal part of their existence. Free love, of course, exists for them in various ways — from absolute promiscuity, to relatively stable marriages. The impression I got was that most stayed attached to another person for anything from a couple of weeks to a couple of years, and then one or the other decided to move on. But even then I was told that it was easier to find a girl to sleep with in the East Village than it was to find a free meal, which was not especially hard in itself.

For the most part — and I can only speculate about this — I think that hippies are a heterosexual group or perhaps mildly bisexual (that is, they'll take a sexual partner of either sex) and that the homosexual hippie is rare indeed.

A great many of society's attitudes about hippies and teeny-boppers (who are also pretty free sexually, judging from those I've talked to) probably stem from our awareness of this aspect of their existence. For example, I talked to some policemen about the hippies, and one said, "Look, let's face it; if I were sixteen I'd be there with them." When I reported this to a hippie, he said, "Sure, all they think about is the free love; but they don't know what the rest of it means at all — the poverty and the religious part of it."

It is essential to our understanding of hippie free love to know that the hippie word for a girl is "chick" — an old word, but one that is subtly depersonalizing. One might have to feel some responsibility towards a woman or even a girl, but towards a chick one has to feel only a kind of impersonal tenderness for whatever time one is with her, and one certainly does not marry a chick. This contrasts explicitly and suggestively with the present practice among Harlem Negroes of calling their girls their "women" or even their "old lady," as though what they are looking for is the kind of motherly security in a woman that one could never find in a chick.

Another aspect of the combination of free love and voluntary poverty is that the usual masculine-feminine roles are dropped. Men no longer feel that in order to sleep with a woman they have to be responsible for her support or the support of her children (hippie girls are supposed to take birth-control pills, because the random production of children is not part of the hippie way of life). Thus, economic responsibility (or non-responsibility) is shared equally. Even after marriage, when the father must go out and find enough money to support a wife and child, he does not have to feel that his masculine ego is especially involved in the process because he does not have to try to prove himself by getting a lot of money to buy a large house and fill it with furniture.

It is, I think, evident to every psychologist and to a large number of ordinary observers that our society has been going through a kind of crisis in the whole matter of the definition of the proper roles for men and women ever since the industrial revolution, when machines that could be tended by women or children began to take over the work traditionally done by men, while women, whatever their problems, still had their traditional functions, those of giving birth and caring for children. The hippies have found in their free love and reduction of sharp sexual definition at least one answer to the crisis.

It is true, of course, that free love is love without responsibility, either emotional or economic, and those who point to the hippies' renunciation of responsibility can point to this aspect of their existence as one more evidence of it. But again, most of these young people are reacting against a suburban life in which the whole concept of responsibility has turned the lives of their parents into gray wastes of meaninglessness. For many people, responsibility towards a spouse means to continue to live with him exclusively long after any emotional reason for doing so has passed. Often this sort of marriage continues "for the sake of the children" — but if the children are beneficiaries of it, they are also the chief sufferers from it. In general, the hippie scene has not been in existence long enough to allow us to tell what will happen sexually to its members. Almost all whom I talked to said they expected sooner or later to find a partner that they will want to stay with for the rest of their lives, and then they'll marry. Only time will tell whether the result will be stable, happy families that carry on on the basis of love rather than "responsibility," or, alternatively, loose, squalid, temporary arrangements, with more unhappiness than pleasure.

The Hippie Ethic

The hippie ethic is simple, and simply put: "Do your own thing, but don't try to put your thing onto anybody else." This, of course, does conflict with their evangelistic attempts to "turn on" other people in society, but apart from that, hippies do seem to live by it. What the ethic means, more precisely, is that each individual must discover what — either for any given day, or for a life — is the activity that most meets his own personal needs and desires, and then he must do that. But it is only to please himself that he must do it, not in order to satisfy some general social requirement or the demands of some other individual. Nor must the hippie demand of any other individual that he conform his life to any pattern that does not intimately suit him. This

65

sounds like a simple, even mindless, formula, almost in-
fantile in its self-gratificatory aspects. But its full meaning can be revealed only in terms of the middle-class
background to which it is a reaction, and it leads directly to an understanding of the hippie's psychological
profile.

Most hippies come from homes haunted by the need
of the parents to spend their lives doing somebody else's
thing. That is, parents are consciously suppressing or
giving up their own most intimate desires in order to
achieve status, to take care of their children, to have a
forty-thousand-dollar house in the suburbs, to avoid
scandal, to rise in the world. In fact, the whole middle-
class meaning of "work" is something that one does not
want to do but does anyway. It is a joyless, grinding
activity, whether it is in the office, in the city, or at
home. The children have, indeed, seen their parents
reach, by means of this "work," the middle-class nirvana.
Parents have achieved the goals for which they have
striven and found that they have dehumanized themselves and are desperately disappointed people. Having
never disciplined themselves to the freedom of doing
their own thing, then, they have in many cases passed on
to their children their own sense of frustration at their
lives; and the children, reversing the pattern of their
parents' lives, have gone out, not in rebellion, but beyond rebellion, to do precisely what their parents have
always wanted to do but have lacked the freedom to do.
They are, in many ways, living out the unlived life-lines
of their parents.

It is true, of course, that for many hippies doing one's
own thing becomes mindless, escapist self-indulgence.
But for many it means creative work, study, reading,

honest attempts at understanding oneself and others. After all, escape, particularly alcoholic escape, is what grows out of spending the whole week doing somebody else's thing, and even drugs are not in themselves a means of escape. Some of the creative possibilities of doing one's own thing were described by Gary Snyder in a conversation between himself, Allen Ginsberg, Timothy Leary, and Alan Watts reported in the San Francisco *Oracle:*

> The anthropological reality is that human beings, in their nature, want to be in touch with what is real in themselves and in the universe.
>
> For example, the longshoremen with their automation contract in San Francisco. . . . A certain number of them have been laid off for the rest of their lives with full pay, and some of them have been laid off already for five years — with full pay — by their contract.
>
> Now, my brother-in-law is a longshoreman, and he's been telling me about what's happening to these guys. Most of them are pretty illiterate, a large portion of them are Negroes. The first thing they all did was get boats and drive around San Francisco Bay . . . because they have all this leisure.
>
> Then a lot of them got tired driving around boats that were just like cars, and they started sailing. Then a few of them started making their own sailboats. They move into and respond to the possibility of challenge. . . . Now, human beings want reality. That's, I think, part of human nature. And television and drinking beer and watching television, is what the working man laid off wants for the first two weeks.
>
> But then in the third week he begins to get bored, and in the fourth week he wants something to do with his mind and his body and his senses.

Snyder's vision may be idyllic, but it does express the

possibility that when men are freed from doing other people's things they will find worthwhile things to engage themselves with. The hippie businesses, the proliferating hippie magazines and newspapers, and the hippie poems, paintings, and sculpture also give evidence that when people are free to do their own things they will not necessarily engage in mindless self-indulgence.

So far as I could tell, the hippies' ethic is allied to their definition of love, for, after all, they do think of themselves as the love generation. Most of the hippies I talked to felt that the "love" in the term "love generation" was really something closer to tolerance and understanding than the more fiercely possessive and passionate love we have associated with the word since the Middle Ages, or the abstract and highly verbal love that Christian churches preach. (No hippie will ever feel compelled to be crucified for anybody else, but he will share with you whatever he has if you want him to.) If they are not political activists, they do oppose the Vietnamese war in the name of their form of love, partly, I think, because they see it as a gross national interference with letting other people carve out their own things. And many of the boys are fiercely opposed to the draft as a form of social compulsion. They even tend to turn the other cheek, particularly in their encounters with policemen, to whom they shout, "We love you," as the policemen cart them off to jail.

Hippie Communities

One of the most interesting developments among the members of the psychedelic generation is the establishment across the country of rural communities where a number of people can drop out in common, and either farm, or create, or just be. Such communes are deliberately tribal. They are being set up so quickly that there is now a tribal-commune coordinating center on Ashbury Street in San Francisco, "to establish a base for the exchange of both information and materials sought by the communities involved." The most pressing need, of course, is for land for people to drop out onto, and the description of the establishment of the coordinating center reads in part: "If you have land to share or donate for the use of people realizing the beauty in communal living, this is what is needed most. We are associated with the Kiva of San Francisco, a non-profit religious organization. Its ultimate goal is to assist the thousands of seekers coming to San Francisco in finding their way back to nature. And the need, of course, is for land in the country — land upon which these voyagers might settle and discover their relationship with the earth."

These communities tend to be leaderless in the sense that they avoid all rigid organization and rely highly on voluntarism; they include men, women, and children, and like the monasteries of the Middle Ages, welcome anybody who wants to drop in (or drop out). In many cases, they practice organic farming (the use of only non-chemical fertilizers) in their need to get as close to nature as possible.

It is particularly, I think, the older members of the movement, like Gary Snyder, Allen Ginsberg, and Timothy Leary (who has his own community in a large house in Millbrook, New York), who recommend such a pastoral, tribal existence. And they talk as though this kind of drop-out will result in people's getting beyond drugs. In fact, one community — artistic, rather than farming — that calls itself Drop City considers drugs unnecessary. An inhabitant, writing of it for *Inner Space*, says: ". . . We are beyond decadence. The only spirituality left in an ascetic society is sensuality. We are sensualists. There are thousands of undiscovered, unnamed senses. We attempt to nurture every one. We try to devote ourselves fully, mind, body, and soul, to whatever we are doing. We try to sing."

In general, these communities are an attempt to establish integration apart from a society that has disintegrated into a mass of lonely individuals, cut off from each other, from the source of their food, from fresh air and water, and even from their own bodies — nudism is practiced in some of the communities. The hope is that in an unspecialized tribal existence, men may come to be *with* each other in harmony and love, without the separateness of caste, class, religion, private property, and a possessive family structure. Some even envision communities of scientists and manufacturers in which progress, research, and exporting can go on. But one must suspect that a primitive ideal, carried out as thoroughly as these are, will result in very little scientific or technological work, which does, after all, demand a detachment from nature.

The real tests of these communities, however, will be their ability to get through the second winter, and their ability to avoid having grow up within them hierarchies of class and ability that will create the same problems that they are planned as escapes from. For example, in a farming community some men are going to be better workers than others — stronger, more diligent, more active and inventive. They must, though, if the community is to retain its ideals, be content to use their abilities to

70

serve the group rather than to aggrandize themselves, and this is a human ideal rarely realized. More importantly, only some years of experimentation will tell just how sexual rivalry and jealousy can be eliminated from communities in which sexual exclusiveness is not a terribly strong ideal.

Perhaps, after all, these communities serve best as the working out of a vision of the good life that American civilization has made increasingly more difficult to live in our cities. In that sense, whether they succeed or not, they have a prophetic function for the rest of us — or perhaps just the function of serving as a locus for some of our wiser fantasies.

A COLLEGE HIPPIE

Fred is no hippie, but he shares many of the attitudes and values of the hippies. He is the best poet in the student body of a private liberal-arts college in the New York City area and is typical of the hippie manqué who is sticking out college. He tends to frequent Tompkins Square Park when he gets a chance, dresses in the casual, hippie manner, marched in the Spring Mobilization for Peace, and has often considered going to live in the East Village as a hippie. He has also seriously considered taking LSD, but one of the deterrents has been some articles in the *East Village Other* describing recent scientific reports that ingestion of LSD may cause chromosome damage and Fred doesn't want to take the chance of begetting deformed children. At root it is his poetry which is the major thing in his life.

I talked to him in my home because he didn't feel that he could talk freely in his own home with his parents

71

around. He brought me his most recent poem, a delicate piece of work about the relationship between a young boy who played at being Davy Crockett and Mr. Riley, a man in his neighborhood who would sit and talk to the boy. It was a good, unpretentious poem, peculiarly American in tone and subject.

Allen Ginsberg is something of an idol to Fred, particularly since he sent one of his poems to Ginsberg, a poem about Ginsberg. The poem was returned with thanks and Fred was advised to forget about Ginsberg and about current affairs and current people and just concentrate on himself — what he was, and what he had lived through and felt like.

Fred has problems with his parents that are more serious than most of the hippies. His father is an old-line Catholic, a second-generation American, who was upset that his son had marched in the Spring Mobilization for Peace because that seemed like a criticism of America. As a result, Fred is in a bind about the draft. He hates the war and in general cannot stand the violence and aggressiveness that mark American society today. He would gladly leave the country and go to Canada — even stay there for the rest of his life — in order to avoid fighting in a war that he thinks is immoral. But he thinks that if he would do anything like that, his mother, who has already had one sick spell because of his general hippieness, would go completely out of her mind. The fact is that Fred feels responsible for the emotional well-being of his parents (unlike a younger sister, who couldn't care less about what the parents think). It is this fact alone, I think, that will keep Fred from ever being a hippie and will create problems for him if he leaves for Canada, or burns his draft card, or applies for conscientious objector status.

Fred is fed up with America for a lot of reasons, and his disgust is intensified by the factory workers that he worked with last summer. They are all traditionalist Catholics, of the sort who have the most intense emotional tensions about other ethnic groups. The Italians despise the Poles, for example, and the Irish despise both of them. But they all unite on two subjects — "longhairs" and "niggers." "Longhairs" and "niggers," they feel, ought to be taken out and shot.

As the son of second-generation Italian-Americans who are not well-off economically, Fred would have been expected, sociologically, to have aimed at one of the accepted, prestige professions in America — physician, accountant, lawyer, engineer, businessman. Then his son would have lived out the repressions that he underwent while he was getting a secure social and economic status in America. Instead, Fred has two occupational goals, to be a poet and a college professor of English, and he is about as close to being a hippie as he can emotionally be. Another alternative for his life would be to move into the mountains and become self-supporting in some way away from society.

If Fred has in fact skipped a generation, he has done so on account of his intellectual brilliance and his idealism, both of which he seems to have gotten from his mother. These are somehow combined in the fact that he remembers having read *The Robe* in third grade. As a sophomore in high school he was a minor seminarian, and by the time he was fifteen he had determined to become a priest and give his life to the church. But having gotten that close to the church, and being that idealistic, he rebelled against it because he was aware of the hypocrisy in it. It was quite simply that the church as a whole and its clergy don't live up to the ideals they themselves preach.

In general, Fred is repelled by organization and labels. He doesn't like, for example, to be called a hippie, or a Catholic, or even an American or a student. Even being called a writer or a poet upsets him. He has, that is, a very clear idea of himself, and no generalizing label fits what he, himself, really is.

His literary tastes are predictable. It comes as no surprise to find him especially interested in Walt Whitman, William Blake, and Ernest Hemingway from among the established writers, and Harold Pinter and Edward Albee from among current playwrights. He also likes Jack Kerouac, who as we shall see stands as one of the major literary figures of the Beat Generation, John Barth, author of *Giles Goat-Boy*, and Ken Kesey, author of *One Flew Over the Cuckoo's Nest*, who is now no longer writing, but riding around the country in a psychedelic bus.

His friends in college, according to his estimate, are a group of about twenty people, and if his acquaintances are lumped to form what might be called his "group" they would probably come to about fifty. That includes the theater set, but he was disappointed when the theater set didn't march in the Spring Mobilization for Peace. Even though he was in the Spring Mobilization and wrote a moving and impressionistic description of it for the college paper, he does not feel politically involved. He feels that he marched, as he puts it, in order "to lend my body so that they could have four hundred thousand people." At one point recently, in fact, he made a decision not to get involved with Catholic Workers in the Bowery. His "thing" is poetry and perhaps a state of being, not political or social activism.

He is not "beyond rebellion." As he says, "I know I'm rebelling, but it's not a blind rebellion. I know what I'm rebelling against."

3.
The Hippie's Drugs

I have a vague memory of a meeting that I went to when I was quite young, perhaps ten or eleven. I think it was sponsored by the W.C.T.U. — at least I know that my attendance there was. The speaker warned us of the dangers of marijuana, telling ghastly stories of people who went wild under the hallucinogenic effect of the drug, who killed their best friends under the illusion that the friend was an enemy, who walked out of windows under the illusion that the floor continued out the window, who stole, raped, and generally became monsters under the influence of the drug. He also told us that men were in the area selling marijuana to school children and that there was a substantial reward offered for anybody responsible for the arrest of a marijuana pusher. I left the meeting in a blissful state of terror and hope. I had never known that there was anything in the world quite so horrible as marijuana and was certain that I would collect the reward for exposing a pusher. Death was too good for him.

Then, a couple of weeks ago, I picked up a pamphlet in a local supermarket entitled "The Truth about Marijuana — Stepping Stone to Destruction." It begins,

IS MARIJUANA HARMLESS? Don't you believe it, not for a single instant. Don't listen to the kooks, to the odd-balls, to a few fuzzy-minded college professors or so-called intellectuals who smugly insist that there's no harm. No harm? Ask the Federal Bureau of Narcotics about that. Ask how the records through the years show marijuana not only becomes habit-forming, but leads eventually to the use of major drugs . . . to heroin, to becoming "hooked," to becoming a *dope addict.*

The pamphlet continues by enumerating items listed under such headings as "murder," "rape," "robbery," and "assault."

Such pamphlets are posted on college bulletin boards for laughs. The fact is that marijuana, for better or for worse, is used by millions of Americans of almost all levels of society, and its use will inevitably increase in the future. Such establishment organs as *Life* and *Newsweek* have run features on marijuana, with *Life* slightly more opposed than *Newsweek* to its use, but mainly on the grounds that it causes people to drop out of society — that is, to refuse to accept the ordinary social standards of behavior and enterprise. *Newsweek's* writers claim that one reason young people smoke marijuana is that it is the single thing about which their parents' generation has most consistently lied. "Pot is not, as its strongest opponents charge," states *Newsweek,* "a menace that leads to drug addiction, sexual promiscuity and violent crime. But neither is it, as its most dedicated advocates believe, an innocent social diversion with no psychic significance." *

On one point *Newsweek* is clearly wrong. Marijuana's most dedicated advocates do not claim that there is "no psychic significance" to marijuana. On the contrary, they tend to claim far too much for the drug. A writer in the *Oracle* says, for example, "Speaking for many who are friends and for myself, I have not the slightest reservation in saying that this much maligned plant has powers

* *Newsweek,* LXX, No. 4 (July 24, 1967), p. 46.

that elevate the human condition from a purely material plane to the spiritual."

Maybe as many as 50 per cent of the students at schools such as the University of California have used marijuana at least once, and students at the school where I teach estimate that about 10 per cent have used it. But hippies and teeny-boppers *all* have used it, and many use it as a background for existence almost as casually as a man might smoke expensive cigars. It is distributed free at love-ins and be-ins, and anyone walking into Tompkins Square Park any evening can smell the slightly sweet odor of marijuana being smoked.

So far as I can discover, one must learn how to get satisfactorily high on the marijuana that is sold in the United States. It is, that is, perfectly possible and even normal to try marijuana for the first time with absolutely no effect, or perhaps a slightly unpleasant effect. The proper way to begin is in company, making a ritual out of it, learning from the others how one ought to react. At best, the general effect is a heightening of sensation, so that one smells, sees, feels, and hears more keenly than before. Jazz musicians used to claim that under marijuana they could more accurately hear every note that was being played by every other member of the band, and music lovers have said that while listening to a symphony under marijuana they could hear all of the instruments separately. These effects may be due in part to the altered time consciousness experienced under marijuana, so that whatever one does seems to be done very slowly. Climbing a set of steps, for example, can seem to take up to half an hour. In almost every case, of course, there is general euphoria and a relaxation of inhibitions. Marijuana does not seem to heighten sexual urges, but it can heighten sexual pleasure if one makes love while on the drug. Not on the whole a very interesting set of good effects, and nobody that I have talked to about marijuana seems to get very excited about it. I myself think that most of the pro-marijuana agitation is more a form of social protest than an expression of real interest in the drug.

Marijuana is not physically addictive. That is, the body never grows dependent on the drug, as it can with heroin, barbiturates, cigarettes, and alcohol. Some people, however, do become psychologically dependent on the euphoric effect of the drug. These so-called potheads, however, are probably clear addictive types who might just as well have grown addicted to sex, television, motorcycles, or tennis, with not much different results. Smoking marijuana can, of course, lead to heroin addiction, but not in the way that the Narcotics Bureau claims. Because the marijuana high is perfectly sufficient — in fact, when a marijuana smoker reaches his high, he always stops smoking, unlike drinkers — and because the smoker does not build up a tolerance for the drug so that he does not keep needing more and more to reach the same high, there is no reason for a marijuana smoker to go on to heroin unless he has already been influenced either by the Narcotics Bureau, his parents, or the pusher to think that marijuana is a way station on the road to heroin.

The purported addictiveness of marijuana and its purported power to cause heroin addiction are really part of a symbol-system of our society. Let us suppose, for example, that we lived in a drug culture, rather than an alcohol culture. Hard liquor, then, would become the heroin of our society, with the person who drinks three martinis at lunch the equivalent of today's mainliner. The alcoholic would become the feared "dope fiend," and there would, of course, be plenty of evidence to show that alcohol is a dangerous and fearsome drug (it is, by the way). Suppose, however, that another, milder drug found its way into the culture, namely Coca-Cola, containing many of the ingredients of whiskey but not, like beer (which is, for purposes of the analogy, merely cut whiskey), containing the same addictive drug. (Coca-Cola does contain caffeine, and does, in fact, give something of a pickup more because of that than because of its sugar content.) Suppose, then, that society, because of certain similarities between the dreaded whiskey and Coca-Cola, decided to ban Coca-Cola and to tell frightful stories about crimes that people had committed after or while drinking Coca-Cola and to impose fearful penalties for its sale or importation. The result would be the growth of a subculture of Coca-Cola drinkers who would furtively sip it, sensitizing themselves to its effects, heightening and coloring the pleasure they got from it, feeling guilty and wonderful. Some would become dependent on even its mild effect, and perhaps more on the subculture in which they drank it. Others would feel, "Now I've crossed the line; I've done the terrible thing, and I might as well go all the way since I'm on the road to addiction and already a criminal anyway."

The analogy is not perfect. Objectively, the effects of marijuana are more intense than those of Coca-Cola. Its ability to release inhibitions have led some people (very few) to aggressive acts while under its influence. But the fact is that the symbol-system of a society has more to do with altering consciousness than marijuana has. And the major effect of marijuana smoking in our country is going to be in the attitude created by social guardians among young people who know from experience the harmlessness of the drug. Further, young people have, for themselves, broken down the symbol-system that puts marijuana and heroin in the same category. Those that I have talked to see heroin as a pathetic accompaniment of ghetto life, dangerous and addictive — in short, not their "bag."

There are, besides marijuana, a number of other psychedelic substances — peyote, mescaline, LSD, and a new, powerful drug called STP that is beginning to sweep the country and is very dangerous by all early reports. Hippies experiment constantly, with ordinary Lipton's tea, lettuce, Sominex, anything, and report their results to the underground press. There is even the banana hash, nothing more than the baked banana peel, or part of it, that is supposed to induce a mild high.

But apart from the proliferation of psychedelic or pseudo-psychedelic substances, the drug that sets hippies apart and is, so far as I can tell, virtually identical with hippiedom is LSD.

In 1943 a researcher in Sandoz Laboratories at Basel, Switzerland, accidently ingested a small quantity of a substance derived from a rye fungus and as a result had "fanastic images of an extraordinary plasticity." The substance, now known as LSD-25, may be of incredible importance to our civilization. During the fifties a great deal of research was undertaken with the use of the drug, first because it was thought that it simulated a schizophrenic state of mind that would allow researchers to study the effects of schizophrenia more carefully, and then for possible therapeutic values. In one set of experiments, for example, LSD seemed to cure alcoholism (though later experiments would indicate that the earlier

81

results were obtained more because of the interest of the researcher than the drug itself). There was research on religious consciousness, and almost invariably subjects given LSD had a greater awareness of God, some even returning to conventional religious practices they had previously given up. In psychotherapy, LSD accelerated cures by allowing the patient to recall repressed material that the psychoanalyst had tried in vain to bring out by conventional methods. Subjects taking LSD considered themselves more creative, more understanding of others, even more in love with their wives. In short, in the whole field of the human consciousness, LSD seemed about as revolutionary as the antibiotics had seemed in a different field a decade before.

In the early 1960's, however, the whole matter moved out of the laboratory into the public consciousness with the dismissal of two researchers in LSD, Drs. Timothy Leary and Richard Alpert, from Harvard University. They were dismissed for using students at Harvard as subjects in their experiments, which were taking on greater and greater religious coloration. That is, for Leary and Alpert, LSD was almost the basis of a new religion, or at least a new mysticism. The present explosion of LSD on the social scene, including, paradoxically, both its severe restriction by the United States government and its wide use among hippies and others, is a result of the Leary episode and Leary's subsequent proselytizing. Leary has fairly recently abjured the use of psychedelic substances — at least publicly — but the tempest he started still rages. One of the key phrases of the psychedelic revolution, for example, is Leary's: "Turn on, Tune in, Drop out." That is, take an LSD trip, then discover what is going on, where the meaning is, and as a result of that, dissociate from the goals and standards of ordinary American society.

There is, of course, absolutely no way to tell how widespread the use of LSD is. All hippies and a considerable portion of teeny-boppers have used it. It in itself defines hippie culture. (Obviously, I am certain that one could find a hippie who has not and does not intend to, use LSD, just as one could presumably find a virgin hippie, if one searched hard enough. But even those who have not used it take their attitudes and values from the LSD experience and situation.) Beyond that, probably about one per cent of the students at the fairly conservative college where I teach have tried it, and at a large university, with graduate students, particularly on the West Coast, as high as 10 per cent might have tried it. The crux of the matter, of course, is not the number that have by this time tried it but the effectiveness of that number in spreading the gospel.

"Spreading the gospel" — I use the cliché deliberately, because the LSD enthusiasts do feel an ethical demand to turn others on. Typical of expressions of this sort is an article in *Inner Space* entitled simply "On Morality." The author writes: "If, as we claim, love is the reason we turn others on in the first place, and the reason others first introduced us to the psychedelic state, then that same reason would dictate that we continue to work to see that people can continue to explore their minds, and in turn initiate their friends." The analogy with Christian proselytizing is clear: if LSD has shown its love for us then we can return that love by introducing others to the blessed lord LSD. It is the underlying motive even behind young people's wish to turn on their parents, or the desire of the girl to turn on a whole meeting of

Jehovah's Witnesses because they are such beautiful people.

The religious component of the LSD trip has been explicitly enough stated by many of the young people I talked to, whose descriptions of their experiences I have already related. There is even a specifically religious body, the Neo-American Church, whose principles include the following: "The psychedelic substances, such as LSD, are the True Host of the Church, not 'drugs.' They are sacramental foods, manifestations of 'The Grace of God,' and of the infinite imagination of the Self, and therefore belong to everyone." Beyond that, propagandizers for the psychedelic drugs are consciously aware of the use of psychedelics in religious observances in the past, particularly among tribes of American Indians and possibly even in the Greek mystery religions.

In general, however, states of ecstasy, no matter how they are induced, are a part of religious practices in many parts of the world and even in evangelical groups in the United States. The Christian ritual, of course, has always been associated with wine, and there is no biblical reason to think that the minute quantity ingested at Communion services in modern times represented a norm for the early church. Indeed, during the first century of Christendom, the Eucharist or Love Feast became on occasion a pretty rowdy affair. Our contemporary blindness to the ecstatic component of religion may be partly responsible for our feeling of scandal at the idea of LSD as a sacrament in a religious exercise.

Perhaps, however, the most intelligent and valid relationship between LSD and religion is that between LSD and Zen Buddhism. For the Zen adept, the highest state of consciousness attainable is the *satori*, a mystical state

in which the ordinary perception of the connections between things is dissolved in order to allow a sense of
perception into "being itself." That is, if our apprehension of reality — through logic and cultural values —
stands between us and absolute reality, then absolute
reality can be discerned only by a dissolution of logic and
cultural values, even including generally accepted ways
of perceiving time and space. Both LSD and Zen tend
to bring their adepts to similar states of mind. The
process in Zen is like a kind of psychotherapy, but its
"enlightenment" or *satori* sounds remarkably like the effects obtained from LSD. A Zen adept has described
Buddhist enlightenment to a Jesuit scholar in the following way: "Enlightenment is an overwhelming inner reali-
zation which comes suddenly. Man feels himself at once
free and strong, exalted and great in the universe. The
breath of the universe vibrates through him. No longer
is he merely a small, selfish ego, but rather he is open
and transparent, united to all, in unity. . . . Indeed, enlightenment does not come from without, but only from
within. The self is delivered through its own effort. . . ."

Compare that, for example, with the reports, described
above, of ordinary young people who had taken LSD —
the sense of unity, of being filled with energy, of feeling
that they were at one with God, the universe, and their
fellow men. Even more explicitly does one leading Zen-
LSD scholar describe a part of his own LSD trip:

Again music — harpsichords and a string orchestra, and
Bach in his most exultant mood. I lie down to listen,
and close my eyes. All day, in wave after wave and from
all directions of the mind's compass, there has repeatedly
come upon me the sense of my original identity as one
with the very fountain of the universe. I have seen, too,

that the fountain is its own source and motive, and that its spirit is an unbounded playfulness which is the many-dimensioned dance of life. There is no problem left, but who will believe it.

For those who object that this kind of religious sense of things has no social relevance, no outlet in any love for others except a love that works itself out in proselytizing, some attempts have been made to relate the LSD experience to the ethical life as we generally understand it. Writing in *Inner Space,* the Rt. Rev. Michael Francis Itkin says, "The time has come for the formation of a band of persons who, in the process of undergoing an inward transformation, find themselves guided by the sense of love of their fellow human beings, to resolutely enter the arenas of social life — the contemporary social, political, and economic arenas — to challenge, resist and finally overcome the institutions of injustice, exploitation, discrimination and violence of our contemporary social order." And this state of mind and action he relates to the use of psychedelics, specifically LSD.

Perhaps, however, the importance of LSD in inducing religious states is not in what people like Timothy Leary and Alan Watts write — they are, after all, highly conscious, articulate people. Rather, we should look to the consciousness of the young people in the parks — of those young people who talked more about God than young people would at, for example, a Luther League or Christian Endeavor outing. Admittedly, not all did. For a few, it was a disappointment; for others, it was a matter of kicks. But for Galahad, and Al, and David, it made God real.

By this point, any reader ought to have violent objections, just as, in a way, I do. First: God, after all, is real, is transcendent (or even if he is immanent, he is not simply a state of mind), and is not to be confused with a drug. I asked most of the young people I talked to about this. And, interestingly enough, they, too, had considered the objection. Their answers to all this were similar. Basically, it was that LSD — or any psychedelic, for that matter — did not put anything in the human consciousness that was not already there. It only opened up an awareness of what was already in the mind. Theoretically, then, if the awareness of God were somewhere in the human consciousness, LSD would block all of those inhibiting factors that had repressed it and allow it to become evident where it had previously not been so. This, indeed, is borne out by the fact that when any person describes his LSD-induced experience he reveals a tremendous amount about himself, his own previous religious attitudes and hopes. The most astonishing example, of course, was Al with his pained palms. Somewhere in his consciousness, or perhaps, to use the language of psychoanalysis, in his unconscious, was an awareness of himself as Jesus Christ. This, then, is what is revealed under LSD. That is why, though I made no formal count of the matter, I found many hippies talking about religion in the formal terms of Christianity — wondering for instance, about the Virgin Birth or about life after death. I even found several who had studied to be ministers or had planned to enter the ministry or the priesthood when they were younger. LSD, in short, had only intensified and brought to a point of emotional involvement whatever was already in the consciousness of the person. And from my own conversations I can feel certain that every young person I talked to who reported a religious LSD experience would confirm this.

The other objection reveals more about the objector than about the use of LSD. That is, we somehow feel that if an ecstatic state is actually induced by the drug, is it really *fair?* We associate ecstatic states with discipline — as in the Zen experience — with hunger, self-mutilation, years of waiting, praying, self-denying. Why should some kid on a Greenwich Village street be able to claim an ecstatic mystical experience just because he ingested a small amount of a drug? An easy answer, though historically correct, is possible. St. Paul's experience along the Damascus Road was an experience that was immediate and given to one who not only did not deserve it but who should, on account of his hostility to the gospel, have been everlastingly denied it. There are, indeed, those who would say that Paul's experience was really an epileptic seizure and therefore of no value. But would any Christian say that?

More seriously, I think that the objection reveals more about our Puritan sense of the fitness of things than anything about the basic religious experience. Where has God or the universe ever put terms to ecstasy? Why do we, therefore, assume that all pleasure, all genuine goods in life, must be paid for? Why, in short, do we not only value suffering but make it a *sine qua non* for any enrichment of life? If God in his mysterious wisdom wishes to reveal himself to those who have not paid for it, by what standards do we object?

In general, my own thought and study on the subject lead me to the assertion that the religious aspect of the use of drugs ought to force churchmen and intellectuals to a careful and soul-searching inquiry into the religious experience itself, rather than attempting to defend themselves against the facts of recent human experience.

One further objection, however, that I share with the hippies themselves: Many of the more articulate and literate point to the Zen experience as justification for their own religious consciousness induced by the drug. I have pointed out to several, however, that nothing in Zen prescribes the use of psychedelics to achieve the mystical state. Furthermore, there is no evidence that any of the Christian mystics used drugs. Is the use of drugs, then, essential to the hippies' religious experiences, and if so, is it essential on account of *their* own weaknesses? They all find the question unnerving, and their answers differ. Some say that LSD is essential to their religious experiences, but say it reluctantly, and others say that it is not, but are equally reluctant. One answer was that given by a young man who worked in a psychedelic shop on Tompkins Square. He pointed out the door to the ugliness and bleakness, the noise and pollution of the city, and said, "In the Orient, they don't have that. There, they can find a place to go and meditate for hours at a time. Here, we're in the city. We have to find some way to blot out all of that." He was, in a sense, being naive about much of the world, and we can, after all, get out into the country. But the generalized noise — in terms of social conditioning and cultural attitudes that we have internalized from our culture — may be too great for any of us to attain to religious ecstasy without some chemical bomb to blast it away.

So far, I have been saying the best about LSD that can be said. If the story were as simple as that, objection to the drug would be merely stupid prejudice. But there are disadvantageous aspects to the use of the drug, and, fortunately, the most serious users of the drug are aware of this. Allen Ginsberg, for example, is shocked by its frequent and indiscriminate use by a number of young people. It is, that is, easily and frequently abused, and its abuse in this way will lead to some entirely unforeseen results. Unfortunately, the research on the drug is now severely limited, particularly research on human beings, and so many of the dangers will remain undiscovered. Here, however, are some:

There is the danger of more-or-less permanent psychosis as a result of ingestion of the drug. Under careful laboratory conditions, only about one out of a thousand users had psychoses lasting over forty-eight hours, but indiscriminate use produces a higher proportion, including a number of people who, as long as six months after having taken the drug, go into psychosis and have to be hospitalized. (Hippies tend to minimize this feature of drug-taking, just as drinkers minimize the dangers of alcoholism, and even when they do talk about it they use such euphemisms as "a bad trip" or "not coming down off a trip.") There are three ways to minimize the dangers of LSD, however, and if research had continued the dangers might have been greatly reduced by this time. One is the recognition that certain psychological and physical types probably should not take LSD. A little is already known about that: in general, rigid personality types, those who cannot tolerate the unfamiliar and the chaotic, are likely to find themselves in trouble. In addition, because the drug does allow deep and emotionally-involving insight into oneself, people who have repressed very strong fears, feelings of inadequacy, or guilt are likely to find an awareness of these too hard to take and so retreat into psychosis. I would personally suspect that the chance of psychosis, or even of a "bad trip," would be increased with an increase in the age of the user. There are very likely other factors, perhaps even factors in the chemical makeup of the potential user, that would make the ingestion of LSD dangerous for him.

The second way to minimize both psychotic reactions and bad trips is by careful preparation for the experience. Books and articles on the subject are fairly common, but the general principle stated in them is the same: LSD renders one extremely vulnerable to one's environment, and therefore one must, beforehand, prepare the environment carefully. There should be a trained "guide," who has had the experience, and whom the user knows and trusts. Interruptions from the outside should be avoided — a sudden trauma could cause psychosis. Music, art, and poetry that the user knows and is fond of should be provided. In fact, from everything that I have read, a carefully prepared and well thought-out trip is *almost always* successful.

Finally, there are a number of chemical antidotes to get a person down from a bad trip. These are duly reported in the underground press, with instructions for obtaining and using them. Some are even non-prescription. With these, not only can psychosis be prevented, but the bad trip, an experience about as unpleasant as the good trip is pleasant, can be terminated easily and quickly.

One of the astonishing things one finds when reading the psychedelic literature is the degree of understanding and sophistication shown by the devotees of the drug with regard to its dangers. The very fact that they are aware of its dangers and ways of minimizing them is some evidence that use of drugs is likely to continue. Of course, LSD, like any drug, will always be abused — it will be taken in too large doses, too often, in the wrong atmosphere, by the wrong person, for the wrong reasons.

There are, however, other partly incalculable dangers in taking the drug that will only show up as the result of findings made over a long period of time. For one thing, because it is a drug it has an inevitable debilitating effect on the human nervous system, just as alcohol or even coffee does. Its very power may mean that this debilitating action is quicker than anybody now knows. A psychologist friend of mine, for example, who has closely observed one prominent evangelist for the LSD cult over a period of years, says that the man has grown less aware, less articulate, in fact, as far as my friend can tell, less intelligent than he was previously. Others can perhaps observe this in the now obviously slurred speech of the same man — and for my part I find many of his recent writings and utterances merely silly and hardly evidence of a lofty academic background.

Another effect, scarcely more tangible, but more amenable to laboratory work with rats, is chromosome damage that results from the ingestion of LSD. (It is a sign of the sophistication of the underground press that the *East Village Other* featured this fact in a recent article.) Allied to that is the fact that rats given LSD during the middle stage of their pregnancy had either deformed offspring or none at all. If such facts accumulate, the psychedelic community will be the first to become aware of them, and they may, more than the possibility of psychosis, spell the end of the use of LSD, though by that time a substitute will probably have been found.

A letter in the *East Village Other* reads as follows:

This letter is being written to enlighten some people

to the FACT that the Hippie and Drug revolution can and did happen to a middle-class suburban area outside of New York City. [My guess is Long Island.]

Most of the hippies age from about 11 to 18 [!], and in many cases, over. Most of the participants are in high school, and quite a few people sell Grass, acid [slang for marijuana and LSD], peyote, DMT, STP, and amphetemines in school. After school, the sort of "hang-out" is a little luncheonette-restaurant, where the hippies frequently buy and sell drugs.

The drug scene started here, about 2½ years ago, with the use of mainly amphetemines and grass. About 1½ years ago, lots of kids (hippies and even a few Hoods) started buying grass and taking peyote. This lasted until about seven months ago (it isn't used so much lately, because of the awful, bitter taste of the button, and also the nausea felt after taking it). Then came acid, which is still going very strong.

There are two main kids who score drugs from the city, and also Mexico. One of them has his mother buying grass and acid from him. Quite a few other kids have their parents turning on, and, if not turning on themselves, the parents have given their kids permission to do so, anyway. Even some household pets (cats and dogs) have taken acid trips.

Mostly at "open parties," drugs are given out, sold and taken. If there is news about a plainclothesman there, (which is rarely!), the mind-blowers are taken BEFORE going to the party. Otherwise, if no suspicious people are there, out come the pipes and pills and smells.

Just recently, a lot of kids have been taking and scoring the chemical drugs, DMT and STP, besides LSD.

Most of the kids are pretty hip and cool about drugs. They figure, "as long as psychedelic drugs and herbs are illegal, we'll keep quiet about it." Also, they aren't influenced by the biology-textbook passage, "Although marijuana is not physically addictive, it is emotionally addictive and it will definitely lead to other dangerous drugs."

Not too many kids here have any desire to even look at heroin, opiates, or other "body" drugs.

We hope that "mind" drugs will be made legal, and other suburban areas will be enlightened to where it's really AT by TURNING-ON.

LSD is not hard to manufacture in large quantities. No doubt sharp high-school students have already found out how to do it in home laboratories. Legal means will not stop the spread of drugs, in the face of the evidence of a letter like this. I must admit that such a letter frightens me, as the father of a child who was eleven in 1967, and another who will be eleven in 1968. I have no ideas about legalization, except one perhaps not too relevant observation. All drugs, including alcohol and tobacco, are dangerous. Perhaps society ought not to interest itself unduly in forbidding people to put themselves in danger, but where is the middle ground between forbidding a substance and exploiting it? That is, if the legalization of mind-changing drugs ever comes about, does this necessarily mean that they will be promiscuously and incessantly advertised, pushed, lied about by those who want to make money from them, almost forced on our young people by a culture that tends either to forbid things or to make money on them? These are questions, of course, not answers, but leaders in our society must arrive at some answers, and arrive at them soon. Before 1943, LSD was an unknown substance. A letter like that above indicates its rapid spread and acceptance, and a good bit of the other evidence indicates that its favorable effects may just balance its dangers. Neither hysterical condemnation nor evangelical "pushing" will provide answers to what we must see not as a "problem" but as a situation that may have as much hope and challenge in it as danger.

Apart from the merely practical aspects of what drugs are, what they do, and what might be done about them, there exist some fascinating and wide-ranging possibilities about what the increasing use of mind-changing drugs in our country may mean. (I exclude heroin and the barbiturates from this, as what in hippie jargon are called "body" as opposed to "mind" drugs. The kids know the difference, and they are right.) What I am about to propose is a hypothesis that will be mistaken in many of its details, and may, in fact, be altogether wrong. But in many respects, it does fit the evidence, not only of the present scene but of history.

To begin with, one must be aware that psychedelics, to most of the hippie generation, exist as a replacement for alcohol. That is, the drug generation is consciously a post-alcohol generation, and the meaning of this can be determined only if we are willing to look at alcohol as a phenomenon to be placed parallel to, if in opposition with, mind-changing drugs. First, what is the general effect of the psychedelic substances? Those who have used them claim for them that they increase awareness, increase perception, break down defenses, that they are, in general, *heighteners* of sensory and emotional experience. This, particularly, is what makes LSD a dangerous drug because under LSD the user is psychically naked, intensely vulnerable to any feelings of guilt or unworthiness he may have, or, alternatively, intensely vulnerable to anything hostile or ugly in his immediate environment.

Any state of ecstasy that is induced is induced on account of this heightened awareness of oneself and of the world.

Alcohol, on the other hand, is actually a *depressant*, creating a lowering of awareness, particularly awareness of feelings of guilt and inadequacy. The apparent heightening effects of alcohol are due, as everybody by this time knows, to the fact that the alcohol suppresses inhibitions, allowing the drinker to act out previously-repressed impulses, which may be poetic or religious, but may just as well be aggressive or illicitly amorous. Alcohol also differs from psychedelic drugs in its hangover effects. Any person who drinks enough during an evening to become exhilarated will suffer for it the following morning. Drug users do not suffer anything like a hangover — on the other hand, they tend to come down off a trip refreshed. Alcohol, then, is suitable for societies or people who feel a need to suffer in exchange for any pleasure or creativity they may have had. Drugs are appropriate for those who do not feel any psychic need for compensatory suffering.

It is, then, a gross mistake to make a naive identification of alcohol and drugs as a pair of twin vices that wicked young people may indulge in. The two substances differ widely in their effects, and if we are at the onset of a switchover from an alcoholic to a psychedelic society this may have important consequences indeed. For alcohol has been pre-eminently the substance that we associate with Europe and Western civilization in general, whereas psychedelic substances we associate with primitive peoples and the Orient. Alcohol, for example, is at points important in the Bible, and wine and drunkenness were constantly present in Greek culture (even as early as the *Odyssey*).

I think that we can characterize Western civilization, as it comes from Jerusalem and Athens, in such a way as to perceive its *need* for alcohol, the "down" drug, if we characterize it as involving a series of tragic separatenesses. First, in Western civilization, man has separated himself from nature. He becomes subject and nature becomes an object to be fought, manipulated, controlled, or merely avoided. The Greek gods were not gods of nature, though they might have evolved from natural elements. And certainly Jehovah is not a nature God; for that matter, one of the terrains in which we see the Israelites most vividly — the desert — is a terrain against which they must constantly fight. Next, Western man is separated from himself, in the sense that he must constantly fight the flesh in order to elevate the spirit or discipline the intellect. And Western man is always tragically separated from his gods, who dwell afar or in the past, who remain unseen, elusive, mocking, commanding, punishing, but almost never offering their devotees the ecstasy of immediate participation and apprehension.

These separatenesses of Western civilization are what make possible our science and technology, perhaps even our literature and art; in short, whatever we think of as human progress can be seen as an attempt to overcome the separateness, to create a new integration. But the strain on the individual can be tremendous, both in terms of repression and in terms of postponing gratification or doing without gratification altogether. Alcohol, then, comes to lower our awareness of the separateness, to give us a false sense of integration, to delude us to the tragic reality of our selves and our nature. This is the social function of alcohol, that it enables man, tragically split off from nature, himself, his work, and his gods, to continue to strive — in the wilderness or through the stormy seas — and build a civilization. The drug-taking societies, in contrast, are given by their drugs a sense of immediate and total participation with themselves, nature, and God, not, indeed, as an illusion that comes from the drug but rather as an awareness of what man really is in primitive societies.

I think, therefore, that the use of psychedelic drugs by large numbers of our young people may well have cultural significance of immense scope, resulting in a new — for us — definition of what man is and what his place in the universe should be. We may in a very real sense become like primitive or Eastern man, not, indeed, abjuring the progress that we have made as a civilization, but going no further except, perhaps, to perfect the automation that will allow us to function as a society without working "by the sweat of our brows."

The unconscious awareness of this is what, I think, lies behind the violent objections to drug use on the part of many of today's authorities who by education and training have so internalized the values of Western civilization that they never question them, and see only that the use of psychedelics threatens what, in essence, they have become.

4.

From Lost Generation
to Love Generation

Even though hippies tend to be unhistorical in their own thinking, they cannot be understood completely except as part of a wave of history. They did not just happen *ex nihilo* in 1962 or 1964, but they have been happening — indeed, since Creation, no doubt — particularly in America since about 1920, as the third in a series of "generations." I think they represent the crest of a wave, its highest and most extreme point, that will either break down upon itself or sweep up onto the shore, making real inroads into our culture.

There have been in America, in this century, three separate self-styled "generations." They are the Lost Generation, the Beat Generation, and finally, the Love Generation. Even this self-consciousness about one's generation is, so far as I know, a new phenomenon, and needs to be considered. To begin with, it is misleading, because new human beings are born at a more or less steady rate each day and there is no point at which one can break the continuum and say, "Here is the end of a generation and the beginning of a new one." Things happen slowly, like the growth of a tree or even a city. Yet for purposes of discourse and understanding man always tries to arrange and categorize experience, to make it stand still in discrete blocks.

For whatever reason, members of the twentieth-century generation are convinced that they somehow coagulate into recognizable groups. That in itself is, of course, a form of historical awareness and an indication of a good bit of sophistication underlying what often seems like naive primitivism. It is also, however, indicative of a sense of communal solidarity among siblings, as though these young people have gathered their peers to themselves and announced their identity as different from the identity of their fathers and mothers. Members of generations are not, in their own minds, initiates waiting to grow up into the adult world of work and authority but are already spokesmen for a group in their own right.

Surprisingly enough, it doesn't matter how small numerically the authentic members of a generation are. Historically they are all that seem to count when we look back to where the youthful action was in a previous time. That is, these self-styled generations do define the style, the hang-ups, the visions, of almost all the young people of their time, and we can perhaps even understand history better by studying them than by studying the official acts and documents of the governments they were, for the most part, rejecting.

In 1948, Jack Kerouac and a friend were sitting around talking about the Lost Generation and the subsequent existentialism, and Kerouac reports that he said, "You know, this is really a beat generation." This is slender evidence for establishing a link, but it at least establishes the kind of self-consciousness that I have been considering. I am going to try, however, to establish links — not necessarily similarities — among the three generations, to show the degree to which they represent a single, elongated wave of history.

By the nineteenth century many of the ideals of Western civilization were under desperate attack from the dehumanizing power of the machine and from the reduction of man by Marx to an economic unit, by Darwin to simply the most recent step on the evolutionary ladder, and by Freud to a being whose reason, rather than being his essential defining principle, was merely the froth on top of a seething volcano of irrational urges. But education, the established church, a genteel literature, rhetoric, and sentimentality managed to give the official ideals some vestiges of life even up into the twentieth century. Boys who went to college before the First World War still believed in a lot of things, and were still able to think about the nobility of man, the democratic ideal, the liberalism that would peacefully transform society into a benign state of well-being for all, the purity of women, and the strength of men. Their beliefs were precarious, and to blame the First World War for the loss of all of them is perhaps something like blaming an isolated piece of police brutality for a ghetto riot. The fact is, however, that the First World War did mark the end of a great many ideals and gentlemanly beliefs. It was a war marked by those twin evils of spiritual decadence: inflated rhetoric ("Save the World for Democracy") and savage brutality.

What succeeded on a popular and collegiate level is now known as the Jazz Age. Women gave up their purity, raised their skirts, flattened their breasts (no symbols of motherhood for *them*), drank, smoked in public, and were proud to be known as flappers. There were wild parties featuring jazz and bathtub gin, widespread if unreal prosperity, a series of scandals and apotheosized sports heroes, a general reaction against anything but the

101

most immediate self-gratification. It was a party lasting for about eight years, and then all of a sudden everybody woke up at once to the cold dawn of depression and spiritual emptiness.

It is, I think, the sense of spiritual emptiness that links the Jazz Age and the Lost Generation. For while the Jazz Age was marked by glamorous mindlessness, a group of American writers and intellectuals had gone abroad to discover for themselves in Europe whatever values seemed gone from America. They did not, of course, find them there, and so drifted back to the United States (with the exception of T. S. Eliot and Ezra Pound). These expatriates included Ernest Hemingway, John Dos Passos, Malcolm Cowley, F. Scott Fitzgerald, William Faulkner, Walter Lippmann, and scores of lesser talents.

The eccentric poetess and salon grande dame, Gertrude Stein, in a conversation gave them the name "Lost Generation," and this remark was used as one of the epigraphs for Ernest Hemingway's *The Sun Also Rises,* along with a passage from Ecclesiastes, saying, in part, "One generation passeth away, and another generation cometh; but the earth abideth forever. . . . The sun also ariseth, and the sun goeth down, and hasteth to the place where he arose. . . ."

This novel, a major document of the era, presents on a superficial reading the gay, swinging, carefree life characteristic of the Jazz Age. The cast of characters is a group of footloose, casual people, bent on simply enjoying themselves, at a bullfight, fishing, drinking, making love casually and frequently. The main female in the novel, Lady Brett, sleeps with three different men in the course of the novel, and is in love with another. Nobody worries about money, which is apparently inexhaustible.

But underneath all of this frantic and indulgent activity is a pervasive sense of meaninglessness. The first key to the meaninglessness is the incessant drinking in the novel. It is a measure of our acceptance of alcohol that this activity probably goes relatively unnoticed until attention is turned to it. I decided to count the pages in which drinking or drunkenness was explicitly mentioned and found that at least two-thirds of the pages in the novel had some mention of drinking in them. The characters were drowning themselves, or some part of themselves that was so deeply wounded that it could hardly be faced.

But what is perhaps more central than the drinking, or at least more profound than the drinking, is the theme of castration in the novel. The hero, Jake Barnes, had received a wound in the war that made him impotent, so that his love for Brett had no sexual outlet, no fulfillment. This wound, however, is meant as a symbol of the spiritual state of all the men in the novel. Something has happened to them to render them impotent, like the steers in the bullfight who try to tame the bulls but are likely to wind up getting themselves gored.

At one point in the novel, Jake is still willing to search for meaning in the traditional religious way. He goes into a church, and there he tries to pray:

> At the end of the street I saw the cathedral and walked up toward it. The first time I ever saw it I thought the façade was ugly but I liked it now. I went inside. It was dim and dark and the pillars went high up, and there were people praying, and it smelt of incense, and there were some wonderful big windows. I knelt and started

to pray and prayed for everybody I thought of, Brett and Mike and Bill and Robert Cohn and myself, and all the bull-fighters, separately for the ones I liked, and lumping all the rest, then I prayed for myself again, and while I was praying for myself I found I was getting sleepy, so I prayed that the bull-fights would be good, and that it would be a fine fiesta, and that we would get some fishing . . . and as all the time I was kneeling with my forehead on the wood in front of me, and was thinking of myself as praying, I was a little ashamed, and regretted that I was such a rotten Catholic, but realized there was nothing I could do about it, at least for a while, and maybe never, but that anyway it was a grand religion, and I only wished I felt religious and maybe I would be the next time; and then I was out in the hot sun on the steps of the cathedral. . . .*

The quest for meaning, however, becomes translated into blind action because meaning does not present itself in the world. *The Sun Also Rises* as a whole is something of a testament of the Lost Generation, with its search for a meaning that it knows it will never find, its heavy, often almost suicidal drinking (in the case of Fitzgerald, his drinking was suicidal), and its tremendous problems with sexuality. Impotence, after all, is only a symptom of a far more serious condition. It is the condition in which a man cannot act effectively because he does not know where he is, nor who he is, nor what is real.

To carry the analogy further, Hemingway's whole output represents just that kind of impotence, rooted in the awareness that once, but no longer, it was possible to know something and to act with purpose, because the uni-

* Ernest Hemingway, *The Sun Also Rises* (New York: Charles Scribner's Sons, 1926), pp. 99-100. Copyright © 1926 by Charles Scribner's Sons. Reprinted by permission of the publisher.

verse did offer some direction in which to travel. And so his stories and novels are filled with a stoical activity — lion hunting, bullfighting, deep-sea fishing — that masks the essential pointlessness of it all. Even Hemingway's own activity of writing was quite clearly, for him, a way to keep going in spite of meaninglessness. And when the wells dried up, when writing just didn't happen anymore for him, he shot himself.

Castration and impotence — and even the "dry land" so important in T. S. Eliot's poetry of this time — are signs of a meaninglessness that comes when the values of a civilization collapse, when belief is no longer possible and action and love seem empty gestures. Sex loses its roots in love and responsibility, and all we can hope for, to Hemingway, is good fishing or, to Eliot, "shantih," the peace that passes all understanding.

The twenties were followed, quite simply, by ten years of depression, by four years of war, and then by a cold war and the threat of atomic annihilation. All of these years of external and more or less tangible crises tended to reduce the anxiety over questions of meaning and purpose in America. In the depression years, for example, the same people who would have been part of the Lost Generation were politically active, some of them in the Communist party, many of the most brilliant, including Hemingway, involved in the Spanish Civil War, the first real confrontation of our time between fascism and Communism. During the years of the Second World War — and there is no evidence that the depression was over before our entrance into that war — the young men of spirit and ideal went into the army, and the emotions of a whole nation were directed to the destruction of the military power of Germany and Japan. Then our country did something better than it had done during the period immediately after the first war: it actively set about helping the defeated and the destroyed nations, and at home it offered massive help to the returning veterans, many of whom returned to school.

But in many ways, the fifties began to prepare the way for the beatniks and, eventually, the hippies. To begin with, the fifties were incredibly stagnant years for young people in college. American arts of all sorts were at a low ebb. American politics had gotten into the hands of a bland father image, who had shown himself incapable of dealing with Senator Joseph McCarthy, perhaps the most dangerous figure ever to have appeared on the American political scene. Idealism took the form of John Foster Dulles, stuffy, pious, and almost always mistaken in his judgments. Fear of nonconformity and general apathy haunted American campuses, and, quite simply, nothing happened until late in the fifties to create anything like a sense of generational solidarity among the young. That was my generation, and rather than drop out, we copped out — copped out, that is, in the sense that we simply prepared ourselves to make our own private security in the world of our fathers.

But during all of this time there was a ferment that I think may have had more effect than anything else on the existence of a new generation of young people prepared to challenge the affirmations of organized society. This was the new breed of college professors. We can take as a typical professor a man who left the army about 1945. By 1950, or perhaps somewhat later, he had gone through college and graduate school and was about ready to teach in a college. For several years he had to work hard to keep up with his field, to get his lectures set, to find his own authentic voice as a teacher — and to avoid being called before the House Un-American Activities Committee. But by 1956 or later, he had found his voice, had tenure, and was ready to become authentic with his students. He also had been reading Hemingway, Camus, Silone, and Blake (who was getting big around this time), and he was in furious rebellion against any of the genteel tradition that was likely still to exist in the persons of his department chairman and his dean. For nobody came out of the Second World War — or even the Korean War, for that matter — genteel. The beaches of Normandy, the foxholes of the South Pacific, and the brothels of Louisville have differing effects, of course, but they do not produce gentility.

The new breed of college professor was not going to object if a student used profanity in a paper; but he was going to insist that the student read the relevant documents, do the necessary experiments, or make the life observations himself and not rely on anybody else's — particularly not the teacher's — authority. But he had also begun his family, made the necessary compromises to attain tenure, bought a house in the suburbs, and was a good bit like the parents of the hippies themselves — that is, willing to pass on his needs for meaning, largely unmet, to his students, and implicitly to invite the students to seek for meaning themselves, in any way possible. This was the generation of teachers who were most bitterly opposed to advertising and materialism, Eisenhower, even suburbia. It was the generation of teachers who wistfully tried to unite their dreams and whatever nostalgia even they might have had for the old gentility in a last-ditch adoration of Adlai Stevenson.

They didn't make it with Stevenson, but in many cases they did with their students, because the beatniks and the hippies are primarily middle-class college sorts, no matter how hard they try to hide it. The insights and new ideas that students get in the first year of college are among the most important things that ever happen to them.

The novel of the Beat Generation was an unpublished but widely-known work during the fifties. It was as though the Beats had their spokesman waiting for them when the spiritual climate of the country was ready, in 1957, for the novel to be published. It was Jack Kerouac's *On the Road*. Like *The Sun Also Rises*, the novel reads on first view like one continual good time had by a bunch of self-indulgent kids. The narrator is Sal Paradise, a thin disguise for Kerouac himself, a wanderer from Paterson, New Jersey, across the face of America. Sal was a former student at Columbia University, as was Kerouac, and much of his life was built around parties in New York or San Francisco, which were reminiscent of the wildest goings-on of the Fitzgerald twenties.

Sal's life is determined, however, by his meeting with Dean Moriarty, a wild, delinquent, irrepressible, rollicker. Dean talked, drank, made love, took on and put off wives, even generated children with the same reckless abandon with which he parked cars in a parking lot or drove across the American continent. Sal saw in Dean something that was distinctively American, or at least something that was distinctively non-Columbia University or Paterson, New Jersey: "[Dean's] 'criminality' was not something that sulked and sneered; it was a wild yea-saying overburst of American joy; it was Western, the west wind, an ode from the Plains, something new, long prophesied, long a-coming (he only stole cars for joy rides)." *

On one level, the novel is an exuberant celebration of life lived at its most intense and most vivid:

> . . . the only people for me are the mad ones, the ones who are mad to live, mad to talk, mad to be saved, desirous of everything at the same time, the ones who never yawn or say a commonplace thing, but burn, burn, burn like fabulous yellow roman candles exploding like spiders across the stars and in the middle you see the blue centerlight pop and everybody goes, "Awww!"**

That is the quality that most people found in the book and that does remain its dominant note, still very much like the old mindless Jazz Age, in the case of *On the Road* so mindless that it didn't matter that Dean Moriarty had dropped babies across the continent to be reared without a father, or that he was in imminent danger of going to jail for five years for stealing a car. For Kerouac's audience it didn't matter because the beatniks were fed up with a society where men had sacrificed everything so that their children could have a respectable father, where the children later simply felt oppressed by the "debt" that they owed the father, and where the suburban ranch house became a kind of prison, after all.

But there are strong motifs in the novel that betray its sadness and sense of defeat. One of them is Sal Paradise's urge to be something other than himself. For some reason, he had to find for his ideal something as far as he could from Columbia and Paterson, and he found it in

---

* From *On the Road* by Jack Kerouac (New York: The Viking Press, 1958), p. 10. Copyright © 1957 by Jack Kerouac. Reprinted by permission of The Viking Press, Inc.

** *On the Road*, p. 8.

the Italian son of a town drunk in Denver, Colorado (interestingly, Dean Moriarty in real life has the good Anglo-Saxon name of Neal Cassady, and he is still riding high with Ken Kesey and his Merry Pranksters, a turned-on group in a psychedelic bus). And that is often not enough.

Finally, the sadness becomes more explicit when the good-byes in the book begin to outweigh the wild greetings and the reckless joyriding across America. "Isn't it true," Sal Paradise muses, "that you start your life a sweet child believing in everything under your father's roof? Then comes the day of the Laodiceans, when you know you are wretched and miserable and poor and blind and naked, and with the visage of a gruesome grieving ghost you go shuddering through nightmare life." *

In all of his writing, Kerouac has the wild abandon that only barely conceals the raw nerve of meaninglessness. Even though he invented the term "Beat Generation," and meant by it a generation that was beaten down, he was later the one that wanted *beat* to be an abbreviation for *beatitude*. He pointed out, for example, that when his picture was taken as the prototype of the Beat Generation he was wearing a cross around his neck, and every publication that printed the picture except the *New York Times* eliminated the cross. He commented on that, "As a matter of fact, who's *really* beat around here, I mean if you wanta talk of Beat as 'beat down' the people who erase the crucifix are really the 'beat down' ones and not the *New York Times*, myself, and Gregory Corso the poet. I am not ashamed to wear the crucifix of my Lord. It is because I am Beat, that is, I believe in beatitude and that God so loved the world that he gave his only begotten son to it."

* On the Road, p. 105.

The other representative literary figure of the Beat Generation is Allen Ginsberg, the poet. Ginsberg is the son of a Paterson, New Jersey, schoolteacher who writes pleasant, competent verses himself, and Allen is better educated than he often allows himself to seem. He has achieved a kind of *guru* status among many of this decade's youth. Ginsberg is not, by any academic standard, a good poet. But his poem "Howl" struck the note that would, along with *On the Road,* define the Beat Generation for itself. "Howl" is written in the free verse "barbarous yawp" that Ginsberg learned from Walt Whitman and perhaps William Blake. And like Whitman, Ginsberg celebrates all of life, especially the forgotten or despised parts of it. The beginning of "Howl" is by now famous, as famous almost as the beginning of the *Canterbury Tales* or "The Wasteland":

> I saw the best minds of my generation destroyed by madness, starving hysterical naked,
> dragging themselves through the negro streets at dawn looking for an angry fix,
> angelheaded hipsters burning for the ancient heavenly connection to the starry dynamo in the machinery of night. . . .[*]

The poem includes an attack on Moloch, a symbol of the ugliness and oppression of modern American life, of "Children screaming under the stairways! Boys sobbing in armies! Old men weeping in the parks!" [**] It ends with a footnote that proclaims the holiness of all of life: "The world is holy! The soul is holy! The skin is holy! The

[*] Allen Ginsberg, "Howl," in *Howl and Other Poems* (San Francisco: City Lights Books, 1956), p. 9. Copyright © 1959 by Allen Ginsberg. Reprinted by permission of City Lights Books.
[**] "Howl," p. 17.

nose is holy! The tongue and cock and hand and asshole holy!" *

The literature of the Beat Generation, then, is a literature of rapturous despair, of a desperate search for innocence and sanctity through sex, drugs, adventuring across a continent, looking at everything with love, and hating everything that denies the human possibility of love. And whereas the despair and impotence of the Lost Generation were communicated in tight, strictly controlled terms, the despair of the Beat Generation was like the bursting of a dam, a wild, insane rush.

Obviously, not all members of the Beat Generation wrote, but those who did were proud of the fact. Those who simply sat in coffeehouses and talked were somewhat contemptuously referred to as "beatniks." Their style, in general, was subdued and sullen, as though they embodied not the beatitude or even the search for it, but the "beat-down" aspect of Beat life. The music of the Beats was jazz, especially cool jazz, and the general style of the Beats was cool, that is, emotionless, as though life had left them with nothing but a set of defenses against emotional involvement. At least one study made of San Francisco's Beats by a psychiatrist showed that 60 per cent would not have been able to succeed in ordinary life, but it's hard to tell what such a study signifies because in America nobody knows what success really means.

At any rate, the "down" Beat, the quiet, sullen coffeehouse sitter, was a dead branch on the generational tree. It was the wild, outgoing, intensely verbal exuberance of a Ginsberg and a Kerouac that succeeded in becoming something slightly different, the hippie. The similarity

* "Howl," p. 21.

between what these men represent and what the hippies represent is illustrated by a statement from Gregory Corso, himself a Beat poet: "The Beat Generation is a generation of love. Not until the sun rejects you do I reject you, this is their love. They aren't violent. To be violent is not to be beat. To be beat is to be hip. Hip means love, means indifference, means not wanting to be bugged or to bug. Hip means metropolitan cosmopolitan solitude, hip means being on a street corner bombed out of your mind." And *On the Road* ends like this: ". . . and nobody, nobody knows what's going to happen to anybody besides the forlorn rags of growing old, I think of Dean Moriarty, I even think of Old Dean Moriarty the father we never found, I think of Dean Moriarty." *

So perhaps in one way or another, the thread that binds together the Lost and the Beat Generations is a search for meaning, that is, the search for the father, or even the search for the Father. This is just as true of the hippies, who can be roughly but accurately defined as the exuberant part of the Beat Generation now high on LSD. It is why when I, a middle-aged "straight" sat on the grass or stood in a hallway talking to any of them, they were desperately anxious to talk, to tell me what it was, what they felt and thought and did, because in some obscure way I represented a father to them.

* *On the Road,* p. 310.

5.
Hippies in History

There is no doubt that by this time the hippies represent a calculable historical fact. That means, to put the matter in its simplest form, that when the cultural history of our times is written, the hippies will not be overlooked even if they are treated as a passing and mildly interesting phenomenon that lasted for only a couple of years. More likely, they will be dealt with as one phase of a recurrent manifestation of the human spirit that has existed since classical times. Their relative importance to culture and civilization, therefore, can be gauged only if we view them alongside similar movements and individuals in the past.

In order to discern the place of hippies in history, I have relied more on intuition than on hard definitions, and the following is in no way an attempt to be inclusive. In general, I have searched for those individuals or groups that voluntarily separated themselves from the prevailing systems and standards of a society in order to find meaning that they could not find in that society. I have included only those also characterized by gentleness and poverty.

The first hippie, then, is clearly Socrates. We know little about the life of Socrates except that he was, at the age of seventy, still walking the streets of Athens, followed by a band of young disciples, careless of the means of life and even of his family. His method and style were radical examination, not of the outer world but of the inner man. "The unexamined life," he said when he was on trial for his life, "is not worth living." And so, like the hippies, he was willing to spend a lifetime examining himself and helping others to their own self-examinations, to the virtual exclusion of all other concerns. He did not even care to write down his thoughts since he was convinced that he knew nothing at all. His whole process constituted, however, a radical critique of a society that had forgotten the ends of its own existence, and of men who had never learned the ground of theirs.

The one thing that may seem un-hippie about Socrates is his relation to society, since he clearly and at all times cared for the laws of his own city, even preferring death to escape from prison. He was proud, in fact, that he had served in his country's army and on its legislative committee. In general, he did not think of himself as a dropout but as a gadfly, bound to sting that great horse, the state, to greater and greater awareness. But there is a strong element of that kind of thought even among hippies, not only the articulate ones like Ginsberg and Leary but also the random samples one meets in the park. They, too, see themselves as offering society a viable alternative to aggressiveness and the rat race.

The final and perhaps the most crucial similarity between Socrates and the hippies is the violence with which "straight" society dealt with both of them — for there is nothing quite so irritating as being told that your life, because it is unexamined, may not be worth living.

The historical setting for Socrates was in some ways similar to our own, that is, it was a period of decayed

115

rhetoric and hollow standards. Socrates was born into a city activated by some of the noblest ideals ever propounded to a society, and in many ways he was one of the last Athenians to have really accepted those ideals — freedom, tolerance, justice, openness, individual worth, participatory democracy. But during the last thirty years of his life, the city gradually, under the pressure of the war with the neighboring city of Sparta, lost all of her ideals. Finally, under the leadership of Cleon, a lowborn demagogue, Athens pursued with unnecessary cruelty a losing war abroad, and at home bribed the poorest class of citizens to support that war.

The second hippie for us, a less charming, less effective figure, is Diogenes the Cynic. Diogenes, who died just eighty years after Socrates, in 320 B.C., may well have taken much of his style of life from Socrates. The legend is that he lived in a tub with a stick, a wallet for alms, and a cloak, which served at night as a blanket.

Diogenes and his followers considered their function in life to be, as they put it, to "deface the currency"; that is, to show up the falseness of the standards and systems by which society lived. His writings are now lost, but we know enough about them to know that they contained passages as shocking to straight society as anything in the underground press — passages, for example, in defense of cannibalism and incest. His voluntary poverty made him self-sufficient, independent of society's help, and fearless of any harm it could do. From this position he and his followers were able to attack the falseness and immorality of their society, and they did so with the aggressiveness and shamelessness of dogs; hence we get the name *cynic*, which comes from the Greek and simply means *dog*.

116

Cynicism had a long life, mainly because it was incorporated into some Christian sects, for the cynic's neglect of the body, defiance of civil authority, emphasis on social reform, and universality merged easily with similar attitudes in early Christianity. In fact, the cynic style characterized many movements, and there is some possibility that its influences are at work in the Desert Fathers, the monastic movement, the heretical sects of the late Middle Ages, the Renaissance, the sects of the Reformation, in the personality and style of William Blake, and finally after a leap across a century in the style and writing of Allen Ginsberg. That is, cynicism in its classical sense may be not just a movement analogous to the hippie movement but a definite source of it. But the demonstration of that line of influence, if it exists, is hardly within the scope of this book.

In a specifically Christian context, we find hippies in the deserts — the hermits. A nineteenth-century historian writes of them: "There is perhaps no phase in the moral history of mankind of a deeper or more painful interest than the ascetic epidemic. A hideous, distorted and emaciated maniac [St. Anthony], without knowledge, without patriotism, without natural affection, spending his life in a long routine of useless and atrocious self-torture, and quailing before the ghostly phantoms of his delirious brain, had become the ideal of the nations which had known the writings of Plato and Cicero and the lives of Socrates and Cato." That is precisely what a member of the genteel tradition might say if he were to observe the hippie scene today. But we are now more sympathetic than the nineteenth century was to spiritual quest, and the facts about the Desert Fathers are not as repulsive as some of their extremes might lead us to believe.

117

The Desert Fathers began "dropping out" about 250 A.D., just when the Roman Empire, already well along in its spiritual impoverishment, had begun its long downhill movement. They left mainly to find a personal integrity that they could not find in the city and they espoused voluntary poverty and asceticism, for the most part, in order to allow themselves to concentrate on those things that were truly important. In other words, it was a search for meaning which they no longer found in society or the more regular forms of church life.

Many of the hermits lived by weaving mats and baskets out of the palm leaves of their desert and it was customary for them to practice the same kind of sharing that hippies practice. Also, hermits were not gloomy, unsociable sorts, as they are often pictured. They did meet with one another and gladly talked to visitors who went out into the desert to see them. Some even met together for religious services. Further, we now know that the hermits valued highly the practice of Christian love; theirs was not an absolute retreat from the world.

Later groups of hermits joined together into cenobitic communities, like the communes of the hippies, and these in time became a source for the monastic movement of the Middle Ages. Ideally, monasticism is a paradigm of Timothy Leary's "Turn on, tune in, drop out" in an explicitly Christian context. That is, the communities became oases of meditation and spiritual integrity, serving society indirectly by prayer and example, and often directly by distributing goods to the poor and offering hospitality to all who came asking for it. The monks were "turned on," of course, by the love of Christ and communion with him rather than by the spiritual state induced by LSD, and they mortified the flesh by denying

118

it rather than by indulging it. But even those differences are less important than the similarities between the two groups.

One of the most important of medieval ascetics — certainly the most appealing — was St. Francis of Assisi. His father was a successful cloth merchant and as a young man Francis was a leader in the good society in Assisi. Only when he went to Rome on a pilgrimage, after having had a vision of Christ, and mingled with the beggars in St. Peter's Square, did he understand that poverty was his vocation. He had an altercation with his father because he had taken cloth from him and sold it to repair a ruined chapel; and so, undressing in front of his father's house, he left, clothed only in a hair shirt and saying, "Until now I have called you my father on earth. But henceforth I can truly say: Our Father Who art in heaven." He then gathered a group of followers and established the Franciscan Order, an order of begging friars who were to own nothing for themselves, not even books, and who were to beg no more than they could consume in a day.

But the St. Francis that appeals most is the St. Francis who lived with the sense of the essential unity of all life, who preached a sermon to his brothers the birds, and who could thank God not only for all living things, but even for Sister Death.

The appropriateness of San Francisco as the city where the hippies are most active is not lost on the publishers of the San Francisco *Oracle*, who, on the back page of a recent issue, have printed a picture of St. Francis embracing the universe, with a bird on his arm and the wolf that he supposedly tamed by his feet. The page, which advertises the "summer of love" in San Francisco, contains St. Francis' well-known prayer, "Lord, make me an instrument of thy peace. . . ." Sacrilege? An article in the *East Village Other* goes one step further:

> Two thousand years ago some beatified rejects from the predominant tribe ran around the Mediterranean preaching love. For this they were persecuted and one of their leaders was hung on a cross by the Romans who thought they were a threat. History proved that indeed they were a threat to the Roman way of life which had become selfish and obsolete . . . . It proved that the Christians had the artistic vision to assimilate their mythic changes in the world's psyche and eventually marry the remnants of the Roman life. Eventually the mentality of greed which was the motivating force behind the Roman Empire took hold again and the Christian revolution was ruined — the Church became a land owner.

Perhaps no more unlikely group has ever tried to appropriate for itself the Christian mantle; but that sort of thing comes with more grace from the hippies than, say, from groups that bear the sword and the torch in the name of Christ.

Moving into the late Middle Ages, again a time of spiritual deterioration in the sense that the system of values and symbols that held a culture together was wearing out, we find a number of heretical sects which in one way or another dropped out of society in order to establish new and different forms in which they could discover meaning.

More specifically, the period from the eleventh to the fourteenth century in Europe marked the breakup of the old feudal, agricultural system and a growing industrialization and urbanization. The social and economic bonds that had given men a sense of a place in society, and the consequent implicit faith in the teachings and life of the church, gave way to the impersonality and insecurity of urban life. Many who had been serfs — virtual slaves, but assured of food and protection — now became part of an army of urban proletariat, restless, discontented, looking for new spiritual masters, and amenable to the preaching of any demagogue who could promise them some imminent kingdom. In their misery and impotence they were especially prone to accept the teachings of anybody who would tell them that they were in some mysterious way better than their masters.

In many ways the situation was analogous to what we find now in southern California and in the urban slums of our country. In both situations men and women exist without any roots or sense of participation in the effective life of their society. Alienated and envious, they join religious bodies that promise instant redemption along with the damnation of whoever does not accept the doctrine or has oppressed the class of the communicant.

This sort of thing was, naturally, much more explicitly Christian during the Middle Ages than it is now, because Christianity has built into it a doctrine concerning the end of the world and a millennium of joy and justice for the saved and damnation for the non-believers. (The same kinds of expectations probably underlie the fulminations of Stokely Carmichael and H. Rap Brown today.) Europe was swept by proliferating sects of millenarians, each with its own charismatic leader and set of beliefs, each opposed to the established church, and each bitterly fought by the church. Those closest to the hippies were a group from the Low Countries, northern France, and the Rhineland known as "The Brethren of the Free Spirit."

The Brethren of the Free Spirit were not all members of a single, monolithic cult, however, so much as they were separated into small bands of like-minded groups who believed and practiced roughly the same things and kept in touch with each other by a kind of underground net of communications (much like the "underground press" of our own hippies). Not only were they fought by the Catholic church — one was burned at Mainz as late as 1458 — but both Calvin and Luther warned against them, or at least against sixteenth-century equivalents.

The Brethren were mystical and subjective. True to their urban orientation, they distrusted authority and system, choosing to rely on their own experiences and intuition. They saw the church either as an enemy or simply as an institution that had outlived its usefulness. For them, the wave of the future would be communities such as theirs — communities that must have been remarkably like the hippie communes. They tended, also like the hippies, to divide men into the "crude" in spirit and the "subtle" in spirit — themselves — and ultimately acquired such an exalted sense of the subtlety of their own spirits that they identified with God, assuming that Christ himself would have been one of them had he lived long enough.

Basically, their theology finds its expression in typically pantheistic statements like "God is all that is," "God is every stone and in each limb of the human body as surely as in the eucharistic bread," "Every created thing is divine." For them the afterlife was the reabsorption of the human soul into the universal soul — God — but heaven could be attained in this life by a recognition of one's own essential divinity. In this mystical, experiential sense of one's own identity with God, the Brethren of the Free

Spirit sounded exactly like a hippie describing his experience under LSD.

The ethical consequences of this position are easily deducible: the Brethren of the Free Spirit evidently practiced free love, not only because those who have identified with God cannot sin but also as a symbol of their freedom from the laws that governed the unsaved. And by the fourteenth century they decided that private property was meaningless, not only because of the notion that everything was God's and therefore no man ought to arrogate anything to himself, but also because of the imminence of the millennium when all property would be shared anyway. They shared all of their own property among themselves, begged, and in some cases stole for their maintenance. Finally, however, there grew up a tendency on the part of the Brethren to exploit others, and there is some indication that from the beginning their free love was exploitative rather than a genuine sharing.

One scholar writes of them: "In the later Middle Ages it was the adepts of the Free Spirit who conserved, as part of their creed of total emancipation, the only thoroughly revolutionary social doctrine that existed. And it was from their midst that doctrinaires emerged to inspire the most ambitious essay in total social revolution which medieval Europe was ever to witness."

The Brethren of the Free Spirit were more important by far than the official history would have them. Their program was probably doomed not because of the hostility of the church and the state towards them, but because society did reorient itself during the Renaissance and the existence of new frontiers in all realms of human endeavor gave men new dreams to dream and a new meaning for their struggles. That is, the revolution came, but not in the form that the Brethren had expected.

It would be interesting to stop this rapid survey of hippie history in the eighteenth century — particularly in England. For that century was a period of rapid industrialization and urbanization, with consequent social uprooting, tremendous growth of an urban proletariat, loss of traditional faiths, anxiety, and spiritual emptiness. This was the period of Swedenborgianism, the Great Awakening in England and America, and Wesleyanism — all movements that relied heavily on experience, particularly experience of a mystical and emotional sort, and all movements that appealed strongly to the lower classes.

It would, further, be interesting to give some special attention to the Shakers, a sect that had its origins in England but quickly moved to America. These followers of Ann Lee, with their experiments in communal living, their dancing, and even their complete celibacy, raise for us questions similar to those we have been considering. They were a turned-on group — drop-outs from society who sought an ecstatic expression for their faith and their unrestricted charity even as they practiced total sexual abstinence. Because they are quaint — even "old-fashioned" — to suggest that they are analogous to the hippies seems preposterous. But if the similarities are hard to discern, it is not so much due to intrinsic differences as to our own inability to penetrate the outer husks of things to see the spiritual drives underneath.

But we shall move on even further to consider William Blake, one of the historical hippies acknowledged by Allen Ginsberg as a spiritual forebear of what we see today: "I rush up enchanted — it was my first sunflower, memories of Blake — my visions — Harlem." * But as similar as Blake was in many ways, none of the hippies that I talked to had any awareness of this figure who grew out of the same milieu as the Shakers. The reason for this ignorance may be quite simple: most well-educated hippies have still had only about two years of college, and Blake is not usually studied until upper-class years.

Blake was born in 1757, and by the time he was twenty he had completed his first volume of poetry. But he had been a remarkable human being long before that, having announced to his mother when he was four years old that he had seen the prophet Elijah sitting in a tree in his backyard. Besides being a mystic and a poet, he was an artist and an engraver, making his living by his engraving, whenever he made a living.

Blake developed a system of copperplate engraving that he said had been revealed to him in a vision from his dead brother. He used this in the publication of his first major work of poetry, a group of delicate, childlike lyrics, *Songs of Innocence*. This illuminated printing, the organic combination of art and poetry, is one of the most characteristic features of at least one of the underground periodicals today, the San Francisco *Oracle*. The *Oracle* mingles text, drawings, and colored papers and inks with the kind of audacity and brilliance not seen since Blake's first experiments. Even the designs in the *Oracle* have the kind of swirling, mystical non-reality that characterizes Blake's engraving.

Also like the hippies, Blake's poetry celebrates the explosive world of the liberated human psyche, pure world-energy, and looks outside the symbols of Western civili-

* Allen Ginsberg, "Sunflower Sutra," in *Howl and Other Poems* (San Francisco: City Lights Books, 1956), p. 28.

zation for its meanings. Blake hated the narrow scientific
vision associated with figures like Locke and Newton;
and he, furthermore, saw Jehovah as a figure of limiting,
damning reason and Christ as a symbol for an art that
can liberate man. And for Blake, liberation meant the
liberation of vital energy, symbolized by all that European, Christian civilization had denied. Thus, in the
name of Christ, Blake worshiped the "devil" as the devil
had been defined by the deluded followers of Christ.
Some of his most radical ideas are contained in a series
of "Proverbs of Hell," a section from a longer work entitled "The Marriage of Heaven and Hell." Here are a
few:

> Drive your cart and your plow over the bones of the dead.
> The road of excess leads to the palace of wisdom.
> Prudence is a rich, ugly old maid courted by Incapacity.
> Bring out number, weight & measure in a year of dearth.
> Prisons are built with stones of Law, Brothels with bricks
> of Religion.

Like the Brethren of the Free Spirit, he believed in sexual
freedom and once asked his wife if he could bring a
mistress into the house to live with them. She refused,
but his poems are full of the praise of the free action of
the passions and the body.

Nevertheless, like the Brethren of the Free Spirit and
the hippies, Blake's interests were not primarily sensual
but spiritual. His engraving, like psychedelic art, was
not a mirror of actuality but a series of visions of an
eternal reality, images of God and the prophets, flowing
up like flames to an ideal sphere. And his most characteristic lines express more beautifully than anything else
just what the hippie seeks in his LSD experience:

To see a World in a Grain of Sand
And a Heaven in a Wild Flower,
Hold infinity in the palm of your hand
And Eternity in an hour.

During his own lifetime, Blake was considered a fanatic or perhaps simply mad, though his friends knew him as a cheerful, rational human being. His poetry, particularly the later, difficult prophetic books, was ignored as the obscure ravings of a madman. But in the last ten or twenty years Blake has come into his own, acclaimed by — of all things — the academic establishment, but also by American students, as one of the greatest of English poets.

The last historical hippie that I shall point to is the one figure most generally recognized by the hippie community, Henry David Thoreau. Just recently a Thoreau postage stamp was issued. It drew the ire of members of the straight community because Thoreau was pictured as bearded, looking like a hippie. In this the hippies agreed with their critics. They rushed out, according to the New York postmaster, to buy the stamps in far larger quantities than they usually buy stamps; and a reproduction of the stamp formed the cover of the *East Village Other* for July 15-20, 1967.

The New England Transcendentalists as a whole — Bronson Alcott, Emerson, and Thoreau — have been enshrined by the academic establishment, which for many students is equivalent to embalmment. Emerson, particularly, is something of a drag — pompous, shrill, and humorless. But his friend Thoreau has somehow escaped to be a constant underground hero. I have never heard

a student say an unkind word about Thoreau and I
have met a number to whom his greatest book, *Walden*,
is something of a Bible, an expression of the human spirit
that speaks clearly and strongly to the most sensitive and
aware of young people. Thoreau speaks in a style that is
direct, slightly ironical, and profoundly masculine. Passages from *Walden* clearly show similarities between him
and the hippies and also help to explain that, beneath
the superficial fact that Thoreau went to live by himself
for two years at a pond near his home town, there was a
profound search for meaning and the wisdom of a rare
human spirit.

The first and most evident similarity is that Thoreau,
not only at Walden but throughout his life, chose voluntary poverty because he had become convinced that men
are more enslaved than liberated by their possessions. It
is, for example, with something of an ironic chuckle that
he details to the penny his expenses of living at Walden,
in order to show just how little a man who is more determined to enrich his soul than to furnish his house can live
on. "Most of the luxuries," he writes, "and many of the
so-called comforts of life, are not only not indispensable,
but positive hindrances to the elevation of mankind.
With respect to luxuries and comforts, the wisest have
ever lived a more simple and meagre life than the
poor. . . . None can be an impartial or wise observer of
human life but from the vantage ground of what *we*
should call voluntary poverty." His voluntary poverty
extended to his taking the same attitude towards dress
that the hippies apparently take.

It might be said, too, that Thoreau lived in terms of
immediate gratification, that insult to a Western civilization which is built, according to Freud, on the bedrock

of repression and postponed gratification. Thoreau did exactly what he wanted to do, and to read his book is to read the work of a supremely happy man. He describes his awakenings as joyful events because each dawn brings him a new day in which to live. There is even a mockery in his description of his life, because he knows that he is writing for straight society. He writes of his life at Walden: "I did not read books that first summer; I hoed beans. Nay, I often did better than this. There were times when I could not afford to sacrifice the bloom of the present moment to any work, whether of the head or hands. Sometimes, in a summer morning, having taken my accustomed bath [in Walden Pond], I sat in my sunny doorway from sunrise till noon, rapt in a revery, amidst the pines and hickories and sumachs. . . ."

His acceptance of all of reality is almost Franciscan in its completeness. He loved Walden Pond with a love that grew from and issued back into a deep knowledge of the pond and its history. He even rejoiced in the buzz of a mosquito, and he spent one whole afternoon being eluded by a loon on the lake in a delightful game of tag that the loon invariably won. Like St. Francis, his religion was a religion of affirmation and praise.

But Thoreau's major similarity to the hippies is his attitude towards society (not towards his fellow men, for whom he had some affection, a bit of humorous contempt, and a great deal of pity but no hostility). For while Thoreau's life was in every respect morally irreproachable — that is to say, he was chaste, sober, paid his debts, discharged his obligations, and broke no laws — he was clearly aware that he had dropped out, had set himself apart from the standards of society, and was, indeed, conducting a guerilla warfare primarily for the benefit of his own soul. "The greater part of what my neighbors call good," he wrote, "I believe in my soul to be bad, and if I repent of anything, it is very likely to be my good behavior." He did spend one night in jail because of his refusal to pay taxes to a state that supported and enforced the Fugitive Slave Act. Though his pamphlet, "Civil Disobedience," is his major treatment of that incident, he does mention the episode once in *Walden*, in an attempt to explain his relationship to society: ". . . Wherever a man goes, men will pursue and paw him with their dirty institutions, and, if they can, constrain him to belong to their desperate odd-fellow society. It is true, I might have resisted forcibly with more or less effect, might have run 'amok' against society; but I preferred that society should run 'amok' against me, it being the desperate party." (That last clause is a choice sample of Thoreau's wit, the counterpart among hippies being something like Galahad's offering to paint the walls of the Ninth Precinct the day after he had been arraigned.)

Thoreau's remedy for mankind was that it should learn to live simply and organically, in the way that he himself chose to live, "by truly Indian, botanic, magnetic, and natural means," as he put it, returning to nature not merely by going out to live beside a pond but more radically and spiritually, in something like a kind of natural mysticism. And like the hippies, he not only made a folk-hero out of the American Indian but also quoted again and again in his book from the Indian scriptures.

Thoreau was not, however, like his friend Emerson, a teacher looking for disciples. His ethic, as opposed perhaps to his metaphysic, was precisely the code of the hippies — let each person find his own thing and do it, and don't try to put your thing on anybody else: "I would not have any one adopt *my* mode of living on any account; for, beside that before he has fairly learned it I may have found out another for myself, I desire that there may be as many different persons in the world as possible; but I would have each one be very careful to find out and pursue *his own* way, and not his father's or his mother's or his neighbor's instead."

Finally, Thoreau pursued self-knowledge as the central fact of his existence, giving the same rationale for going to Walden Pond that the hippie does for leaving society, for taking up voluntary poverty in Haight-Ashbury or the East Village, and even for taking LSD, in itself a most un-Thoreau kind of behavior. "I went to the woods because I wished to live deliberately," Thoreau wrote, "to front only the essential facts of life, and see if I could not learn what it had to teach, and not, when I came to die, discover that I had not lived. I did not wish to live what was not life, living is so dear; nor did I wish to practise resignation, unless it was quite necessary. I wanted to live deep and to suck out all the marrow of life, to live so slenderly and Spartan-like as to put to rout all that was not life. . . ."

History, for the most part, is the record of revolutions that have succeeded in becoming orthodoxies. The societies and people presented here can never, by their very nature, become orthodox, but this is no necessary reason why they are any less important in understanding the vicissitudes of the human spirit. Admittedly, they are all somewhat foolish, somewhat childlike, if not even childish on occasion. They have contributed little to the "progress" of mankind and have succeeded in no way that our present society would recognize. They were almost uniformly childless, with the exception of Socrates, who placed much greater store on giving birth to ideas than on taking care of the natural children that he had begotten. They were not "responsible" members of society in any sense that would get them named as chairmen of community funds. They tended, on the whole, to be unwashed and physically unattractive. The present vogue of some of them, among members of the establishment, is due more to misunderstanding than understanding. (It is grotesque, for example, to *make* a student read Thoreau, or to erect gilded statues of St. Francis, or to make Blake engravings a book club selection.) They were mostly in trouble with authority and the social majority, and they would be still if they were alive. But they do represent, in spite of variations in sexual conduct, the pure life of the spirit, and that ultimately is what the hippies really mean when they want to be called the "love generation" or "flower children."

6. Beyond Rebellion

Before discussing what it means to go beyond rebellion, one must inquire into the meaning of rebellion. Perhaps rebellion has its classic statement in the speech that Milton in *Paradise Lost* gave to Satan in hell. Satan had rebelled against Christ's being placed higher in the hierarchy than he, and having been cast down from heaven with the rebel angels who followed his leadership he said:

> What though the field be lost?
> All is not lost; the unconquerable Will,
> And study of revenge, immortal hate,
> And courage never to submit or yield:
> And what is else not to be overcome?
> That Glory never shall his wrath or might
> Extort from me. To bow and sue for grace
> With suppliant knee, and deify his power
> Who from the terror of this Arm so late
> Doubted his Empire, that were low indeed. . . .

The tone of the rebel, that is, is filled with violence, hatred, and stoic determination to fight to the death. And the rebel, like Satan, is really trying to replace the master with himself. The rebel is, in short, living and fighting in terms of the categories of the thing he rebels against. He becomes not a different sort of person but a reversal of the enemy — Satan is a god turned inside out so that he still is caught in the same system. That is why a hippie, for example, judging that speech, would simply say that the speaker is uptight about something or other.

More concretely, it is our generation — the generation over thirty — that rebelled against its parents, or against

133

Victorian restraints. Our rebellion takes its forms in the son of a Republican becoming a Democrat, or the daughter of a W.C.T.U. president becoming an alcoholic. Homosexuality is a form of rebellion as is promiscuity. And blatant atheism is simply religiosity turned into its reverse. The rebel, then, still lives on the same axis, within the same general system, as those he is rebelling against. He is much less free than he thinks, because the rebel, like Satan, can see no alternative either to acceding to a given system or to rebelling against it.

Maybe it is precisely *because* the generation of the parents of the hippies — and the activists of the "New Left" for that matter — did rebel that young people today can go beyond rebellion and find their own thing. If we persist in trying to see what is happening as simply a matter of conventional teen-age rebellion we will miss all the inner meaning of it. Instead of defending ourselves against what is happening, we must open ourselves to the human possibilities that our children are working out for themselves. This chapter, then, will be a discussion of areas in which young people today are finding their own thing and inviting the rest of us either to share it or at least get off their backs so that they can live it.

There is, I think, a tendency to exaggerate the differences between the *via activa* and the *via contemplativa* of today's young Americans, two "ways" referred to in the introduction to this book, as though activists and hippies look at each other with mutual contempt. In my own conversations with both groups, I have found a great deal of sympathy and understanding because both were aware that many of the premises on which they work are similar. A hippie-activist dialogue is possible, just as a hippie-Hell's Angel dialogue was possible, and if each side is authentic, they will ultimately find at bottom that they are similar in more ways than they are different.

There is one other postulate on which this chapter will be based. That is that the "beyond rebellion" generation has permeated the general culture and will continue to do so. We are all immensely interested in hippies — today one cannot look at a magazine rack without seeing an article on LSD or hippies — partly because we recognize that part of us is hippie, and we are prepared to allow the hippies to open up options for living that we have kept closed. Beyond that, dress styles, art styles, music, morals, language, education, and even vacations are all in many ways going to be influenced by these kids. The young people I have talked to, for example, have taught me a tremendous amount about even my squarest students. And so, in writing about the general tendencies of the "beyond rebellion" generation, I am writing about all of our children, and about the shape of the future as well.

THE SYSTEM

All of the young people that I've talked to have in one sense or another opted out. They refuse to fashion their lives according to the system of values that they see as dominating our culture. In a sense, then, their strongest unifying force is what they term alternatively the "system" or the "establishment." I have already written a great deal about the failure of suburbia because these kids are for the most part products of middle-class culture. Beyond this, what they see in America is a society that is profoundly discouraging. Part of their disillusionment with the ordinary political process may be that in

John F. Kennedy they were given a glimpse of what might have been, and the present is too hard to take. For no matter what one's politics, one must admit that the spectacle of the richest, most powerful nation on the face of the earth being governed by Lyndon B. Johnson is a testament to something like the failure of a system.

The system has failed in other ways, too. Some activists, from the vantage point of utterly detached philosophy, can approve of the Vietnamese war as the symptom of a neurotic world in the waning stages of sickness, but the young people that I talk to are sickened by it. The single fact of napalm, for example, a substance by which we burn villages containing women and children, is enough to make young people opt out. Beyond that, the war creates a conflict for many of our most sensitive young men, young men for whom fighting for one's country could still have been an ideal that was capable of commanding their energy and their loyalty if the war had been one that they considered just. But for these men, that is no longer a clear and unambiguous way of proving their manhood. So they either must find other ways of being a man or else redefine for themselves the meaning of manhood, perhaps in some way which substitutes moral courage for physical courage.

The riots in the tragic summer of 1967 are further evidence of the failure of the system. Even though the hippies are not politically active, the New York hippies were enough aware to take food into Newark after the riots. As far as they are concerned, a society that can sustain affluent, all-white suburbs as well as ghettoized central cities has somehow failed in human compassion. Stretching beyond that, however, is the whole race situation. America has, up until now, signally failed in achieving

136

full human status for its Negro citizens. A society in which our current racial chaos can exist is a society that has failed its best ideals.

There are indications other than the public and political that convince young people to try to set up alternative systems. While it may be an underground fact, it is still a fact that the family does not function today as a viable social institution. One evidence of this is that the criterion for people going into psychotherapy is not need but the ability to pay and awareness of a problem; and most of these problems are rooted in marriage, with the children as the victims. The index to the failure of the family is not the number of divorces; it is the number of marriages that stay together out of apathy and desperation.

All of these failures — and many others — in our present society have been documented time and again by social scientists and journalists. Now, with the advent of television, they are instantly and vividly communicated to everybody. One can object, of course, that those young people who refuse to accept the values of the dominant society are unduly jaundiced, that our society has, in fact, a number of favorable aspects — freedom, mobility, open opportunity, the availability of the good life to an increasing number of people. But if this is the case then it is also true that even the standards and the style of press and television are problem-oriented, that Negroes who live comfortably in suburbia do not make the newspapers, that those who use Molotov cocktails in Detroit do. And the situation again becomes that of young people responding to the frustrations and the stimuli of their elders, who are not really content, either, but who don't have the keys to get out.

KNOWLEDGE

The young people of this study are in various subtle ways anti-intellectual, or, more precisely, a-historical. That is, they do not intellectualize about what they are in order to understand it in terms of a large historical or systematic scheme. This in itself would not be unusual, because the ordinary American is equally a-historical, and the mass media are as well. But these are in many cases our sharpest and most aware young people. To be sure, this anti-intellectualism is not the sort that is openly contemptuous of learning or of intellectuals — that would be rebellion; it is rather the sort that opts quietly for values unrelated to the reflective, academic life.

This aspect of the present "generation" is profoundly disturbing, at least to me, and yet it fits in with many of the discussions that academicians are likely to have among themselves. Until recently, the ideal of the "liberal arts" was the dominating ideal of American education. The underlying principle of the liberal arts is that man liberates himself from living blindly in an environment that grows out of the past by understanding and thus transcending that past. For example, if our ideals of individuality and free inquiry have grown out of the Greek experience, then the student, to understand the source of these ideals, should study the Greeks rather than simply live with blind assumptions. So, too, we live in a world that is increasingly determined by the facts of science; thus to be a free man — that is, to be able to participate intelligently in the decisions that affect one — one ought to understand the inner workings of the scientific dialogue. This hope, that man can live freely in terms of knowledge of the discoveries and ideals of the past, is what lies under most "core curriculums" in American colleges.

But academicians as well as students are beginning to despair about the possibility of any single individual ever again being able to gain the amount of knowledge that would allow him to function as a free individual, on top of, not smothered under, his world. As a result, men more and more — particularly if they are highly conscious — are aware of their partiality, of the degree to which, as specialists, they must surrender to a kind of fate that sweeps them along unrelentingly.

The rejection of knowledge as a means of attaining wholeness and freedom, then, cannot be seen as simply "know-nothingness"; it is more likely an exploration of appropriate alternative means of becoming fully human. The appropriateness of these means may well consist in the fact that as more and more information becomes stored in computers, available to everybody for instant retrieval, the computer will become that extension of the human brain that will take over the knowing function, leaving the brain free to engage in more immediate, self-gratificatory activities.

One other aspect of the new style in knowledge is perhaps even more basic and extends to kinds of awareness other than intellectual. Western civilization has always seen things in linear, mechanical terms; that is, the essential relationship between events in the world, from the time of Aristotle, has been understood as moving directly from cause to effect, in a chain of consequence. This is not necessarily the way things happen in the world, of course; it's just the way the ordinary man sees them, and it's the way knowledge is organized. But increasingly science, especially physics, has been looking at events quite differently — as fields of force, or in terms of a bundle of interdependent systems. Much of the Einsteinian revolution, for example, must be seen as just that sort of thing. The historical knowledge, then, that forms the basic framework of the liberal arts tradition, is linear. By rejecting history as a means of apprehending reality, young people today are rejecting the linear way of thinking; they are not rejecting knowledge, and certainly not reality.

One can see several forms their alternatives take. One is the way a conversation is often carried on by some young people. More often than not a conversation is a series of observations, phrases, and images laid beside the observations, phrases, and images of the other member of the dialogue. It is, in a sense, a pattern, a series of fields. Part of the field, too, and perhaps the most important part, is the whole context, including the emotional aspects, of the talk. Some of it grows out of experience in places like Harlem, where there is no great amount of rational, linear conversation but where there is a tremendous amount of communication.

The LSD experience, too, is non-linear, and it cannot be communicated in rational verbal sequence. Time and space are destroyed as vital categories under LSD, and totally new forms of apprehension take their place. And yet the LSD user does not consider himself out of touch with reality — he is just out of touch with certain ways of looking at reality. This is why the new art forms, particularly the new forms that music takes, are possibly true reflections of the LSD experience. Traditional Western music is organized linearly, for the most part, with melody and rhythm, but the new pop music is represented with everything going on at once — all of the senses stimulated, no melodic interest, and lyrics that curl back on themselves. Shades of Marshall McLuhan!

Finally, the traditional demand for *postponed* gratification is based on some sense of rational cause and effect, some feeling that things do travel in predictable lines and that if we give up the present there will still be a future. The demand for *immediate* gratification grows out of a different sense of things, the feeling that it's all here now, baby, and you've got to get it all or just not get it. This demand is as characteristic of the activists as of the hippies. Service must be performed now, and the life one lives must be lived now, among the people whom you serve. Activists, that is, do not talk much about the future — theirs or society's. This sense of the importance of the present moment may be laid to the bomb, of course, and that explanation is attractively obvious. I think it is too simple, though the necessity of the past generation to come to terms with the bomb may well have a good bit to do with it. (That is, I think that whatever influence the bomb has on today's young people has come indirectly and subliminally as it were from their parents and teachers.)

Today's radical young people are not just anti-knowledge. In what may be a very effective way, they may be creating new styles of knowledge for the rest of the century.

COMMUNITY

Ultimately, what best characterizes and unifies all of the young people dealt with in this study is the search for community, a search that has, I hope, been evident throughout the book. Community, in its most basic sense, is a grouping that gives meaning to the individual lives within the group. It is the community that sets up sanctions, demands, and rewards; it is the community that punishes and that approves us, and the most serious breakdown in a civilization is really nothing more than a breakdown of the sense of community. When that happens the individual feels separated from the standards by which he feels guilty or at ease, as though effective parts of his life are somewhat outside him. A community can be as small as a family, or it can be as large as a nation; its size is not important. What is important, however, is that individuals in the community accept and share its values; for, ultimately, community is what one dies for.

The hippies are more and more seeing their lives in terms of community, whether a community consists of ten people in a two-room apartment, a commune in the country, the group around the Haight-Ashbury area, or the whole hippie venture, united by their underground press. The evidence of the community consists in the similarity of their language, their style of life, their drugs, and their spiritual adventures.

There is no doubt that the new trends are a response to a breakdown on all levels of a sense of community. Academically, the split between professor and student, particularly in universities, has never been greater. The family, as I mentioned before, simply does not provide the kind of meaning that it is meant to provide. Nationally, the very fact of greater and greater insistence that people fly flags and otherwise display their sense of belonging to America is one evidence that a real, instinctive sense of belonging to the American community no longer exists. This is especially poignant because our history begins with a group of people who split off from the Old World to come to a new land where they could establish a community of meaning. But we cannot live forever on a bank of meaning established at Plymouth. And finally, the church, once the prime institution in society where people could unite for meaning, no longer serves that function except for a few sects which are usually a couple of generations behind today's young people.

The search for community is, of course, a constant event in human history. Some of the ugliest blots on the American cultural landscape are institutions that have searched for community on the basis of superficial resemblances and exclusiveness. These include the segregated, discriminatory fraternities and sororities in American colleges (now simply pathetic vestiges, though their members don't know it), the "exclusive" (no Jews, Catholics, Central or Eastern Europeans, or non-whites) suburban developments, the exclusive country clubs, and the like. They never did work because they were based on merely divisive attitudes among people and not on anybody's essential humanness.

On the other hand, the search for community among young people today is based on the deepest part of man's awareness — his compassion, his self-understanding, even his suffering. It is this, above anything else, that puts the young today beyond rebellion, that means they are not simply fighting the old standards but establishing new ones, that even means they are not simply "copping out," which is negative, but are "dropping out," which can be positive when it implies an attempt to find something to drop back into. Where the genuine attempt to establish community prevails over more temporary attitudes and activities, there, I think, our young people have something to offer American society.

And what can the middle-class, middle-aged square do about it, anyway? We (for I include myself among that group) can begin by trying to understand that nothing a human being is or does can be understood apart from the most basic human motives and needs and that the most important things about hippies and draft-card burners and tough community organizers in the inner city are not their differences from the rest of us but their similarities. Next, we can learn to listen to them, because they are not really fighting us; nobody in search for community is really looking for a fight. Nor do they want to exclude us. If they are looking at the deepest level for some meaning in life, they are looking at a level at which any man can participate. And finally, we can look again at our own institutions to see where the radical criticism of these institutions implied by the young people of this study really has relevance.

Suppose, for example, that the churches again became resorts for community, where people could become radical in the sense of getting at the real root of things with honesty and mutual acceptance, where real love flourished. Suppose, to put it more concretely, the church were a place where hippies and teeny-boppers, political radicals, some Harlem heroin addicts, and a sprinkling of middle-class straights could all talk out their feelings and desires, in perfect, loving honesty, and all would feel accepted. If that would happen, even the church would have returned to what it once was. That is the sort of thing that many young people today are implicity offering us.

SOME BIBLIOGRAPHICAL NOTES

There is one basic work which has been of immense help in the preparation of this study: John Gruen's *The New Bohemia,* published by Grosset & Dunlap in 1967 and described by a reviewer for the *New York Times* as "The Intelligent Square's Guide to the East Village."

Concerning drugs there is a growing literature, but much of it is either too technical or too polemical to be of real help to the ordinary reader. Perhaps the most objective and readable account is Peter Laurie's little volume entitled simply *Drugs,* published in 1967 by Penguin.

There have been other works which have aided in the preparation of this book: on the Beat Generation, *A Casebook on the Beat,* edited by Thomas Parkinson and published by Thomas Y. Crowell Co. in 1961; on the Desert Fathers, Helen Waddell's *The Desert Fathers,* an Ann Arbor Book published in 1957; on the heretical sects of the late Middle Ages, *The Pursuit of the Millennium* by Norman Cohn, a Harper Torchbook of 1961; and on Zen Buddhism, Heinrich Dumoulin's *A History of Zen Buddhism,* translated by Paul Peachey and published by Random House in 1963.

Type, 10 on 12 and 9 on 11 Caledonia
Display, F-26 Phototype and Caledonia
Paper, G. M. Antique